ideals

Food Processor
COOKBOOK

by Barbara Grunes

Ideals Publishing Corp.
Milwaukee, Wisconsin

Introduction

The arrival of the food processor
has revolutionized the art of cooking.
Experts and novices alike have
discovered that this machine
eliminates the time-consuming
preparation that some recipes require.
A day of chopping, mincing, and slicing
is easily replaced with just the push
of a button.
Best-selling author Barbara Grunes
fully understands the capabilities
of the food processor and shares a
complete collection of mouth-watering
recipes that are quickly prepared with
this innovative kitchen tool. All of
these kitchen-tested recipes prove
beyond a doubt that the food processor
has earned a well deserved place in
today's kitchens.
Expand your cooking horizons with the
Ideals Food Processor Cookbook and
start planning the spare time you'll
have when you use this modern
cooking marvel.

Cookbook Editor
Julie Hogan
Food Stylist
Susan Noland
Artwork by
Duane Weaver

Cover Recipes
Old-Fashioned Strawberry Cream Puffs, 60
Gazpacho, 20
Bolognese Sauce, 36

ISBN 0-8249-3006-1

Copyright MCMLXXXI by Barbara Grunes
All rights reserved.
Printed and bound in the U.S.A.
Published by Ideals Publishing Corporation
11315 Watertown Plank Road
Milwaukee, Wisconsin 53226
Published simultaneously in Canada.

Contents

Food Processor Basics

Standard Food Processor Accessories

Following is a brief description of the standard equipment as it relates to the bulk of food processors on the market today. Study the operating manual that comes with your machine to learn the capabilities of the model you are using.

Base

The base encloses the motor and therefore should not be immersed in water. To clean, wipe with a damp sponge.

Work Bowl and Cover

The Work Bowls vary slightly in size and design from machine to machine, but all are made of heavy, durable plastic. Consult your operating manual to learn if your Work Bowl is dishwasher safe.

The Cover seals the Work Bowl while the machine is operating. The Cover has a Feed Tube through which food is added to the Work Bowl. Liquids and dry ingredients such as flour and sugar can simply be poured in; solid foods are eased through the Feed Tube with the Pusher.

Pusher

The Pusher is made of plastic and fits snugly into the Feed Tube. It is used to guide food through the Slicing or Shredding Discs. The pressure on the Pusher determines the thickness of the processed food.

Steel Blade

This blade is used most often for chopping, mincing, grinding, puréeing, and mixing. Food to be processed with the Steel Blade should be cut into uniform 1- to 1½-inch pieces.

The Steel Blade should be handled by the center knob; the blades are extremely sharp.

Practice operating the machine with a quick on-off action. It takes only seconds to process most foods. If the machine runs too long, the food will liquefy.

Plastic Blade

The Plastic Blade is similar in shape to the Steel Blade but is used less often. It is used for softer foods, such as egg salad, tuna salad, and purées.

Slicing Disc

The Slicing Disc is used to slice vegetables, cheeses, fruits, and cooked or partially frozen meats. It also coarsely shreds cabbage.

To prepare food for slicing, cut a thin slice off one end. Cut food to fit the Feed Tube. Stand food upright in the Feed Tube. Process, emptying the Work Bowl often so that processed food does not interfere with slicing. *Always* use the Pusher to guide food through the Feed Tube. Never use fingers to push food through the Feed Tube.

Shredding Disc

The Shredding Disc shreds food into long or short lengths. Load the Feed Tube vertically for short lengths and horizontally for long. Press the Pusher with firm, steady pressure. As with the Slicing Disc, empty the Work Bowl often. Use the Pusher to guide food through the Feed Tube.

Optional Blades

Other blades such as a fine shredder, ripple cutter, French fry cutter and others are available for many machines, depending on the manufacturer.

Storing Blades

Blades and discs should be handled with extreme care. Store blades out of the reach of children. Many manufacturers have attractive holders in which to store blades.

Techniques for Food Processing

FRUITS

Apples   **To Chop** Peel (optional), core, and quarter apple(s). Insert Steel Blade. Add apple(s) to Work Bowl. Process no more than three large apples at a time, using the On-Off control or pulse technique.

To Slice Peel (optional), core, and cut apple(s) to fit the Feed Tube. Insert the Slicing Disc. Stack apples horizontally into the Feed Tube for perfect slices. Process with firm pressure.

To Shred Peel (optional), core, and cut apple(s) to fit the Feed Tube. Process with firm pressure.

To Purée Peel (optional), core, and slice apple(s). Insert the Steel Blade. Place apples in the Work Bowl. Process until puréed.

Bananas   **To Slice** Insert the Slicing Disc. Cut bananas in half crosswise. Stand banana halves upright in the Feed Tube, cut side resting on the Slicing Disc. Process with light pressure.

To Purée Insert the Steel Blade. Cut bananas into 1-inch pieces. Place up to 3 bananas in the Work Bowl. Process to desired texture. Scrape sides of Work Bowl as needed.

Candied Fruits   **To Chop** Insert Steel Blade. Add ⅓ to ½ cup flour or sugar (subtracted from the recipe you are using) to the Work Bowl. Add candied fruits. Process to desired texture. (See photo on page 7.)

Coconut   **To Shred** (Only recommended for heavy-duty machines. See operating manual.) Remove inner and outer fibrous covering of fresh coconut. Cut coconut to fit the Feed Tube. Insert the Shredding Disc. Fit coconut into the Feed Tube. Process using heavy pressure.

To Double Process For finer coconut, empty the Work Bowl after chopping. Insert the Steel Blade. Process shredded coconut until the desired consistency.

Dried Fruits (Apricots, Pitted Prunes)   **To Chop** Freeze dried fruits. Cut into ½-inch pieces. Insert the Steel Blade. Place dried fruit in the Work Bowl along with ⅓ to ½ cup flour (subtracted from the recipe you are using). Chop to desired consistency. (See photo on page 10.)

Lemons, Limes, Oranges   **To Slice** Use seedless varieties, if possible. Choose sizes to fit the Feed Tube. Slice a thin piece from the end of the fruit so that it will stand level in the Feed Tube. Cut fruit in half vertically. For neater slices, load the Feed Tube from the bottom. Insert the Slicing Disc. Use medium to firm pressure to slice. (See photo on page 10.)

To Grate Remove fruit rind. Insert Steel Blade. Place ⅓ to ½ cup sugar or flour (subtracted from the recipe you are using) in the Work Bowl. Add rind. Pulse three times with the On-Off control. Run machine nonstop for 10 to 15 seconds, or until desired texture.

Peaches   **To Purée** Remove peach pits. Insert the Plastic or Steel Blade. Use up to 2 cups of fruit. Process until puréed, 30 to 40 seconds.

Pineapple   **To Slice** Remove the top of the pineapple; discard. Quarter lengthwise; core. Insert the Slicing Disc. Fit the pineapple vertically into the Feed Tube. Process with firm pressure.

To Chop Prepare pineapple as above. Cut into 1-inch pieces. Insert the Steel Blade. Add pineapple to the Work Bowl. Process 2 cups of pineapple at a time. Process until desired texture.

VEGETABLES

Cabbage

To Chop Core cabbage and cut into 1-inch chunks. Insert the Steel Blade. Place up to 1½ cups cabbage in the Work Bowl. Process until desired texture.

To Shred Cabbage can be shredded two different ways:

1. Core cabbage and cut into Feed Tube-size wedges. Insert the Slicing Disc. Fit cabbage into the Feed Tube. Process with medium pressure.

2. Prepare cabbage as above. Insert the Shredding Disc. Wedge cabbage into the Feed Tube. Process with heavy pressure.

Carrots

To Slice Peel and trim carrots. Cut into 4-inch lengths. Pack vertically into the Feed Tube. Insert the Slicing Disc. Process with medium pressure. For thicker slices, increase pressure.

To Chop Peel and trim carrots. Cut into 1-inch pieces. Insert the Steel Blade. Add up to 1½ cups carrots to the Work Bowl. Pulse until desired texture.

To Shred Peel and trim carrots. Cut into 4-inch lengths. Stand carrots in the Feed Tube. Insert the Shredding Disc. Process with medium pressure. If carrots lodge under the disc, stop the machine and rearrange carrots before continuing.

To Purée Use steamed or cooked vegetables that have been cut into 1-inch pieces. Insert the Steel Blade. Process up to 3 cups vegetables at a time. Add ¼ cup liquid, such as bouillon, cooking juices or milk for each cup of vegetables. Process until desired consistency. Add more liquid, if necessary.

Celery

To Slice Cut celery into 4-inch lengths. Remove outer strings, if desired. Insert the Slicing Disc. Stand celery in the Feed Tube. Process with medium pressure.

To Chop Cut celery into 1-inch pieces. Insert the Steel Blade. Place up to 1½ cups celery in the Work Bowl. Process to desired texture.

Cucumbers Zucchini

To Slice Peel, if desired. Slice in half lengthwise, if too wide for the Feed Tube. Seed, if desired. Fit cucumber vertically into the Feed Tube. Insert the Slicing Disc. Process with light pressure.

To Julienne Use small cucumbers or zucchini. Prepare as for slicing. Fit vertically into the Feed Tube. Insert the Slicing Disc. Slice with medium pressure. Remove slices. Stack slices 2½ to 3 inches deep. Wedge tightly into the bottom of the Feed Tube with cut edges at right angles to the Cover. Insert the Slicing Disc. Carefully replace Cover on Work Bowl. Slice. (See photos on page 10.)

Eggplant

To Slice Peel eggplant (optional). Quarter medium-size eggplant lengthwise. Fit quarters into Feed Tube. Slice with light to medium pressure. Sprinkle slices with salt. Drain for 20 minutes. Rinse with water and pat dry before using.

Mushrooms

To Slice Clean mushrooms and stems. Insert the Slicing Disc. To obtain uniform slices, alternately place mushrooms on their sides in the Feed Tube. Process with firm, steady pressure. (See photo on page 10.)

To Chop Clean mushrooms. Insert Steel Blade. Place up to 2 cups mushrooms in the Work Bowl. (Small mushrooms may be

Continued on page 8.

An Illustrated Guide to Food Processing

The food processor makes quick work of chopping, whether it's fruits, vegetables, meats or nuts. Vegetables are cut into chunks and dropped through the Feed Tube with the motor running.

The above photo illustrates the grinding of meat. To do so, use lean meat that has been trimmed and cut into 1-inch chunks. Place in the Work Bowl. Pulse to chop as desired.

Dried and candied fruit are chopped with the Steel Blade. Flour or sugar from the recipe is added to keep the fruit from sticking to the blade.

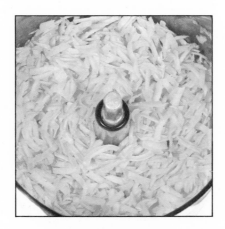

Grating is accomplished with either the Steel Blade or the Grating Disc, depending on the texture of the food to be processed. Note the difference between grated soft cheese on the left and grated hard cheese on the right.

Vegetables and semisoft cheeses are good candidates for shredding. Both make attractive garnishes. To shred, insert the Shredding Disc and position the food in the Feed Tube. Use the Pusher to apply pressure.

Puréeing is basically an extension of mincing and chopping, since it is done with the Steel Blade. Use cooked vegetables or fruits along with added liquid. See individual listings for specific instructions.

Continued on page 10.

put in whole; halve medium-size mushrooms; quarter large mushrooms.) Pulse 3 to 4 times for a coarse chop; more for a finer chop.

Olives

To Slice Insert the Slicing Disc. Stand 5 to 6 olives vertically on top of the disc beneath the Feed Tube. Place the Cover carefully on Work Bowl. Process with medium pressure.

To Chop Insert the Steel Blade. Add up to 1½ cups pitted olives to the Work Bowl. Process until desired texture.

Onions

To Slice for Onion Rings Use small whole onions. Peel and cut off ends. Insert onion into the bottom of the Feed Tube. Replace the Cover. Insert the Slicing Disc. Process with firm pressure.

To Slice Peel and cut off ends. Slice in half through the root end. Fit vertically into the bottom of the Feed Tube. Slice with firm pressure.

To Chop Use medium-size onions. Peel and quarter. Insert the Steel Blade. Place up to 2 onions in the Work Bowl. Pulse 2 to 4 times or until desired texture.

Onions, green

To Slice Clean and trim green onions to 4 inches in length. Stand in the Feed Tube, white end down. Pack the Feed Tube tightly. Process with firm pressure.

To Chop Clean and trim onions. Cut into 1½-inch pieces. Include green tops, if desired. Insert the Steel Blade. Add up to 1½ cups onions to the Work Bowl. Pulse 5 to 6 times or until desired texture.

Peppers

To Slice Cut pepper in half vertically and remove the seeds. Insert the Slicing Disc. Stand a single pepper half upright in the Feed Tube. Use light pressure on the Pusher.

To Chop Quarter peppers and remove seeds. Insert the Steel Blade. With the processor running, drop the pepper through the Feed Tube. Process 1 to 2 times for a coarse chop; more for a finer chop.

Potatoes

To Slice For whole slices, use potatoes that will fit the Feed Tube. Clean potatoes. Peel, if desired. Cut the tip off one end of the potato to make it stand on the blade. Insert the Slicing Disc. Insert a potato into the bottom of the Feed Tube. Process with firm pressure. Potatoes will self-feed, but slices will be irregular. If potatoes are large, quarter and load from the bottom of the Feed Tube.

To Shred Clean potatoes as above. Insert the Shredding Disc. Fit into the Feed Tube. Process with firm pressure. Place shredded potatoes in cold water to prevent darkening. Drain thoroughly before using.

Tomatoes

To Slice For whole slices, use small, firm plum tomatoes that will fit into the Feed Tube. If using large tomatoes, cut horizontally in half. Fit the tomatoes into the Feed Tube through the bottom. Process with medium pressure.

To Chop Quarter tomatoes. Insert the Steel Blade. Pulse 2 to 4 times or until tomatoes are desired consistency.

To Purée Insert Steel Blade. Add quartered tomatoes to the Work Bowl. Process until puréed.

MEAT AND POULTRY

Fish, Raw

To Chop Use only fillets. Cut fish into ¾ to 1-inch pieces. Insert the Steel Blade. Place up to 2 cups fish in the Work Bowl. Pulse 3 to 4 times or until desired texture.

To Grind Chop and then process nonstop for 3 seconds.

Fish, Cooked

To Chop Bone Fish. Insert the Steel Blade. Process up to 2 cups fish at a time. Pulse 2 times or more for a finer chop.

Luncheon Meats

To Slice Cut meat into Feed Tube-size pieces. Place in freezer until firm but not frozen. Process with medium-heavy pressure.

Sliced, Packaged

To Julienne Stack several pieces. An 8-ounce package works best. Roll up meat and wedge into the bottom of the Feed Tube. Insert Slicing Disc. Process.

Uncooked

To Chop Insert the Steel Blade. Trim excess fat. Cut meat into cubes no larger than 1 inch. Place up to 2 cups meat in the Work Bowl. Pulse 2 times, then process nonstop until desired texture, about 7 seconds.

To Slice Cut meat into Feed Tube-size pieces. Place in freezer until meat is firm but not frozen. Insert the Slicing Disc. Insert meat into the bottom of the Feed Tube. Process with heavy pressure. If meat lodges under the Disc, stop machine and rearrange.

CHEESE

Hard, such as Parmesan and Romano

To Shred Cheese must be at room temperature. Remove rind. Cut cheese into ½-inch cubes. Insert the Steel Blade. With the machine running, drop the cheese through the Feed Tube. Process to desired texture.

Medium-hard, such as Cheddar, Mozzarella, Provolone, Swiss

To Shred Chill cheese before processing. Cut into pieces to fit the Feed Tube. Insert the Shredding Disc. Process with light pressure.

Semisoft, such as Feta, Roquefort

To Crumble Chill before processing. Cut into ½-inch pieces. Insert the Steel Blade. Process up to 2 cups of cheese at a time. With the machine running, drop the cheese through the Feed Tube. Process until crumbled, 5 to 7 seconds.

HERBS AND SPICES

Garlic, Gingerroot

To Mince Peel and clean garlic or gingerroot. Cut gingerroot into ½-inch pieces. Insert the Steel Blade. With the motor running, drop the garlic or gingerroot through the Feed Tube. Process until desired texture, about 5 seconds.

Parsley

To Chop Rinse and pat dry with paper toweling. Trim ends. Insert the Steel Blade. Add up to 2 cups parsley, but never less than ¼ cup. Process until desired texture.

Oregano, Basil, Thyme, Rosemary, Mint

To Chop or Mince Rinse and pat dry with paper toweling. Trim ends. Insert dry Steel Blade. Add up to 2 cups, but never less than ¼ cup, herbs to the Work Bowl. Process until desired texture.

Continued from page 7.

Slicing is quickly done in the food processor. The thickness of the slice is determined by which disc is used and the pressure that is applied. See individual instructions for slicing various foods, pages 5 through 9.

The julienne cut is illustrated in this photo and the photo on the right. The food is first sliced as directed and then loaded into the bottom of the Feed Tube and sliced again.

The second slicing results in perfectly julienned foods.

Some foods, such as carrots and celery, are food processor naturals, since they easily fit into the Feed Tube. Those foods that are not naturally straight must be trimmed into Feed Tube-size pieces.

To slice mushrooms, arrange them alternately in the Feed Tube as shown. Apply light pressure on the Pusher to guide them through the blade.

Lemons, oranges, limes, and onions can be fitted into the bottom of the Feed Tube. Carefully attach the Cover to the Work Bowl to avoid dislodging the food. Meats can also be loaded in this manner. Slice only partially frozen meat.

What the Food Processor Will Not Do

It will not process very hard, whole spices, such as nutmeg, peppercorns, and cloves.

It will not process hardened brown sugar.

It will not grind coffee beans.

It will not beat egg whites to the volume of an electric beater.

It will not whip cream as an electric mixer would.

It will not mash potatoes. They become sticky.

It will not slice hard-cooked eggs.

It will not shred lettuce or onions.

It will not process solidly frozen meat.

It will not crush ice.

Processor Do's and Don'ts

Do handle all blades and discs with care to avoid injury.

Do unplug the machine when not in use.

Do keep blades out of the reach of children.

Do use the pushbutton controls to operate the machine. Never use the cover release mechanism.

Do process only the amounts of food indicated. If necessary, process food in two batches.

Do watch the processor closely while operating. It's easy to overprocess food in just a second.

Do familiarize yourself with your machine. Read the instruction manual thoroughly before operating.

Do not operate the machine without the Cover.

Do not remove the Cover until the machine has come to a complete stop.

Do not, under any circumstances, use your fingers to guide food through the Feed Tube. Always use the Pusher.

Do not interchange blades between unlike machines.

Do not overfill the Work Bowl. Keep utensils out of the Work Bowl when operating.

Adapting Existing Recipes to the Food Processor

Family favorites can be adapted to the processor once you understand the machine's basic functions. The primary difference between preparing food with the food processor and using conventional methods is that foods are not processed in the order they are used, but in the order that requires minimum cleaning of the Work Bowl. Because ingredients such as garlic and onions are intensified in flavor during processing, try using less at first.

The equivalent amounts of a variety of foods are given on the next page to aid you in adapting recipes to the food processor.

Following is an example of how to translate a recipe into processor terms:

Conventional Recipe

½ cup minced onion
1½ cups chopped tomato
1½ cups sliced cucumber
1 cup chopped green pepper
1½ pounds ground beef
2 cups bread crumbs

Becomes

Adapted Recipe

1 small onion
2 large tomatoes
1 medium cucumber
1 medium green pepper
1½ pounds beef, chopped
4 slices bread, crumbed

Processor Equivalents

FRUITS

Type of Food	How Processed	Approximate Yield After Processing
1 medium apple	Sliced	¾ cup
1 medium banana	Puréed	½ cup
8 large strawberries	Sliced	1 cup
½ cup nuts (almonds, walnuts, pecans)	Chopped	½ cup
Zest of 1 medium orange	Grated	3 tablespoons
Zest of 1 medium lime or lemon	Grated	1 to 1½ teaspoons

VEGETABLES

5 to 6 large mushrooms	Sliced	1 cup tightly packed
2 medium tomatoes	Chopped	1 cup
1 medium green pepper	Chopped	¾ to 1 cup
1 medium cucumber	Sliced	1¼ cups
3 medium ribs celery	Sliced	1¼ to 1½ cups
½ medium head cabbage	Sliced or Shredded	3½ to 4 cups
1 medium potato	Sliced	¾ to 1 cup
1 medium onion	Sliced or Chopped	½ cup
1 green onion, including top	Chopped	1½ tablespoons
1 medium carrot	Chopped or Grated	½ cup

HERBS AND SPICES

½ cup parsley sprigs	Chopped	½ cup
2 cloves garlic	Minced	½ teaspoon

CHEESE

2 ounces Parmesan	Grated	½ cup
4 ounces Cheddar	Grated	1¼ cups

MEATS AND CHICKEN

1 pound raw beef, pork, veal	Chopped	2 to 2½ cups
1 whole chicken breast, about ½ pound	Chopped	1 cup

BREAD

1 slice fresh bread	Minced	½ cup crumbs

Salmon Paté

Makes 4 cups.

- ¼ cup pitted ripe olives
- ¼ cup snipped parsley, rinsed and patted dry
- ½ cup butter, melted
- 1 15-ounce can salmon, drained, boned and broken into chunks
- 2 tablespoons lemon juice
- ½ teaspoon salt
- ¼ teaspoon white pepper
- 1 cup heavy cream, chilled and whipped

Insert Slicing Disc

Place olives randomly in Feed Tube; slice with light pressure. Set aside.

Insert Steel Blade

Add parsley; mince. Add butter, salmon, lemon juice, salt, and pepper; pulse 3 times; then run nonstop until puréed. Remove to a large mixing bowl.

Fold whipped cream into the salmon mixture. Fold in olives. Pack the paté into small crocks or a tureen. Refrigerate overnight. Remove from the refrigerator 1 hour before serving. Serve with fresh bread or crackers.

Stuffed Mushrooms

Makes 12 servings.

- 2½ pounds medium to large mushrooms, stems removed and reserved
- 1 medium onion, quartered
- 3 tablespoons butter
- 1 slice dry white bread, torn into 6 pieces
- ½ cup blue cheese, room temperature, cut into ½-inch pieces

Insert Steel Blade

Place mushroom stems in the Work Bowl; chop; set aside. Add onion; mince.

Melt butter in a 12-inch frying pan. Add chopped mushrooms and onion; sauté for 3 minutes. Place mixture in a large mixing bowl. Place bread in the Work Bowl; process into crumbs. Add onion-mushroom mixture; blend well.

Add cheese to Work Bowl; process into crumbs. Add cheese to mushroom mixture; blend well. Lightly butter a large baking sheet. Spoon fill-

ing into mushroom caps. Preheat oven to 375°. Bake mushrooms 20 minutes or until filling is bubbly.

Paté with Pistachios

Makes 8 servings.

- ¾ pound veal, cut into ¾-inch pieces
- ¾ pound pork, cut into ¾-inch pieces
- ½ pound chicken livers, cleaned and gristle removed
- ½ pound pork fat, cut into ½-inch pieces
- 3 cloves garlic
- 1 medium onion, quartered
- 3 tablespoons butter
- 2 eggs, lightly beaten
- ¼ cup brandy or white wine
- 1½ cups pistachio nuts, shelled and skins removed
- ½ teaspoon each of thyme, allspice, cinnamon, salt, and pepper
- ½ pound sliced bacon, blanched

Insert Steel Blade

Place veal in the Work Bowl; mince. Place veal in a large mixing bowl. Add pork to Work Bowl; mince. Add to veal. Add chicken livers to the Work Bowl; mince. Add to the minced meats; combine. Add pork fat to Work Bowl; process 15 seconds. Add to meats. Wipe Work Bowl dry with paper toweling. With the machine running, drop the garlic through the Feed Tube; mince. Leave garlic in the Work Bowl. Add onion; mince.

Heat butter in a large frying pan. Add garlic and onion; sauté for 2 minutes. Stir in meat mixture. Stir in eggs, wine, nuts, and spices. Remove from heat. Preheat oven to 350°. Drape bacon slices over the bottom and up the sides of a 4-cup terrine. Spoon meat mixture into the terrine; smooth top. Fold bacon strips over the top. Cover terrine with aluminum foil. Place terrine in a pan that is 2 inches larger. Pour in 2 inches of hot water.

Bake for 1½ hours, until juices run clear; drain. Cool to room temperature. Chill overnight. Serve from the terrine or unmold onto a serving plate. Serve with thin slices of bread and cocktail-size pickles. Paté can be stored for 1 week tightly wrapped.

Shrimp Paté

Makes 8 servings.

 1 medium onion, quartered
 4 tablespoons butter
2½ pounds small shrimp, shelled and deveined
 1 tablespoon dry sherry
 4 sprigs parsley, rinsed and patted dry
 3 cups heavy cream
 1 teaspoon salt
 ½ teaspoon white pepper
 ½ teaspoon ground nutmeg

Butter a 9 x 5 x 3-inch loaf pan. Preheat oven to 300°.

Insert Steel Blade

Add onion to the Work Bowl; pulse 5 times. Remove from Bowl; set aside. Leave steel blade in place. Heat butter in a large frying pan. Sauté onion for 2 minutes. Add shrimp; sauté until shrimp are done. Remove shrimp from heat; cool. Sprinkle sherry over shrimp.

Add 2 cups of shrimp to the Work Bowl; mince 8 to 10 seconds. Remove from Work Bowl and set aside. Repeat until all shrimp are minced. Place shrimp in a large mixing bowl. Wash and dry Work Bowl.

Insert Steel Blade

Add parsley; mince. Add parsley along with remaining ingredients to shrimp; blend thoroughly. Pack mixture into prepared pan. Cover with oiled aluminum foil. Place pan in a larger pan; fill outer pan with 2 inches of water. Bake 1 hour and 10 minutes or until paté is set. Cool to room temperature. Refrigerate until ready to serve. Unmold onto a serving platter. Slice and serve.

Onion Pie

Makes 8 servings.

Crust

1¼ cups unbleached all-purpose flour
 ½ teaspoon salt
 6 tablespoons butter, room temperature, cut into ½-inch pieces
 6 to 8 tablespoons milk

Insert Steel Blade

Place flour, salt, and butter in the Work Bowl; process until mixture resembles coarse cornmeal. With the processor running, pour milk through the Feed Tube. Dough will gather around the center post. If necessary, add more milk, 1 tablespoon at a time, until dough gathers. Turn dough out of Work Bowl; gather into a ball. Wrap in plastic wrap; refrigerate for 20 minutes. Roll out dough on a lightly floured board. Fit into a 9-inch pie plate. Preheat oven to 350°. Prick bottom of piecrust with the tines of a fork. Bake for 15 minutes. Cool.

Topping

 2 large onions, quartered
 5 slices bacon
 2 eggs
 1 cup sour cream
 ¼ teaspoon salt
 ⅛ teaspoon white pepper
 ⅛ teaspoon caraway seed

Insert Slicing Disc

Place onions in the Feed Tube; slice with light pressure; set aside.

Fry bacon until crisp; drain and crumble. Reserve drippings and reheat. Add onions and sauté until soft. Remove onions with a slotted spoon; set aside.

Insert Plastic Blade

Place eggs in Work Bowl; combine 8 seconds. Add onions, bacon, sour cream, salt, and pepper; combine 10 seconds.

Preheat oven to 375°. Pour mixture into crust; spread to edges. Sprinkle caraway seed over top. Bake for 35 minutes. Cut pie into bite-size pieces. Serve hot.

Stuffed Edam Cheese

Makes 12 servings.

 ¼ cup pecans
 1 pound Edam cheese
 ¼ cup beer
 1 tablespoon butter
 ½ teaspoon Worcestershire sauce
 ⅛ teaspoon Tabasco sauce

Insert Steel Blade

Place pecans in the Work Bowl; chop; set aside.

Slice the top off the cheese. Carefully scoop out the cheese, leaving the red coating intact.

Add cheese to the Work Bowl, along with chopped nuts and remaining ingredients; blend thoroughly.

Spoon the mixture into the reserved shell. Cover with plastic wrap. Refrigerate for 1 hour before serving. Serve with crackers or raw vegetables.

Salmon Steak Tartare

Makes 6 servings.

- 3 extra large eggs, hard-cooked
- 1 medium onion, quartered
- 1 pound skinned red salmon filets, cut in 1-inch pieces
- 3 anchovy filets
- ¼ teaspoon Tabasco sauce
- ¼ teaspoon Worcestershire sauce
- 3 tablespoons lemon juice
- ½ teaspoon salt
- ¼ teaspoon white pepper

Insert Steel Blade

Place eggs in Work Bowl; chop. Add onion to the Work Bowl; mince 5 seconds. Add salmon; chop finely, 8 to 9 seconds. Add anchovies, Tabasco sauce, Worcestershire sauce, lemon juice, salt, and pepper; combine. Process until puréed.

Shape salmon mixture into a ball. Cover with aluminum foil. Chill until ready to serve.

To Serve

- 1 medium lemon, ends removed
- 4 sprigs parsley, rinsed and patted dry
- 2 medium onions, quartered

Insert Slicing Disc

Fit lemon into the bottom of the Feed Tube; slice and set aside. Mince parsley; set aside. Add onions to the Work Bowl; chop. Garnish with lemon slices, parsley, and onion. Serve with dark bread.

Mousse of Pike

Makes 8 servings.

- 4 sprigs parsley, washed and patted dry
- 1 medium onion, quartered
- ½ teaspoon crushed tarragon
- 1 envelope unflavored gelatin
- ½ cup warm water
- 2 pounds pike filets, cooked, cooled, and flaked
- 1 cup heavy cream, whipped
- 1 cup Green Mayonnaise (Recipe on page 27)

Insert Steel Blade

Add parsley to Work Bowl; mince. Leave parsley in the Work Bowl. Add onion and tarragon; mince. Remove to a large mixing bowl.

Dissolve gelatin in the warm water. Let stand for 5 minutes.

Add fish to the Work Bowl, 2 cups at a time; mince about 8 seconds. Remove from Work Bowl and set aside. Process remaining fish.

Combine fish with parsley mixture. Fold in cream and mayonnaise. Pour into an oiled 9 x 5-inch loaf pan. Cover with aluminum foil. Chill until set, about 4 to 6 hours. Unmold onto a serving platter. Slice and serve.

Steak Tartare

Makes 8 servings.

- 2 cloves garlic
- 1 medium onion, quartered
- 1½ pounds sirloin steak, cut into ¾-inch pieces
- ¼ cup red wine
- 1 tablespoon lemon or lime juice
- ⅛ teaspoon Tabasco sauce
- ⅛ teaspoon black pepper
- ½ teaspoon dry mustard
- 1 egg yolk
- 1 2-ounce can anchovies, drained
- 1 3-ounce jar capers, drained
- ½ cup gherkin pickles

Insert Steel Blade

With the machine running, drop the garlic through the Feed Tube; mince. Leave garlic in the Work Bowl. Add onion to the Work Bowl; mince. Leave garlic and onion in the Work Bowl. Add beef; mince. Leave beef in the Work Bowl. Add wine, lemon juice, Tabasco, pepper, mustard, and egg yolk. Process just to combine. Mound mixture onto a chilled serving plate. Garnish with anchovies, capers, and pickles. Serve chilled with thinly sliced dark rye bread.

Roquefort Mousse

Makes 8 servings.

- 1 envelope unflavored gelatin
- ⅓ cup warm water
- 4 green onions, cut into 1-inch pieces, including tops
- 8 ounces Roquefort cheese, broken into 1-inch pieces
- 1½ cups heavy cream, chilled and beaten until soft peaks form
- 1 teaspoon Worcestershire sauce
- 6 sprigs parsley, rinsed and patted dry

Lightly oil a 4-cup mold. Sprinkle gelatin over water; stir to dissolve gelatin. Let stand 5 minutes to soften.

Insert Steel Blade

Place green onions in the Work Bowl; mince. Leave onions in the Work Bowl. Add cheese, 1 cup of the whipped cream, and the Worcestershire sauce; pulse until blended, about 8 times. Blend in remaining cream and gelatin.

Pour into prepared mold. Cover with aluminum foil; chill for 6 hours or overnight.

Insert Steel Blade

Place parsley in the Work Bowl; mince.

Unmold mousse onto a serving platter. Garnish with minced parsley. Serve with grape clusters and apple slices.

Paté in Aspic

Makes 10 servings.

- 1 10½-ounce can condensed consommé
- ½ cup water
- 2 envelopes unflavored gelatin
- ½ cup white wine
- 1 medium onion, quartered
- ½ cup butter
- 1 pound chicken livers, gristle removed
- ½ teaspoon salt
- ¼ teaspoon ground nutmeg
- ¼ teaspoon ground cinnamon

Combine consommé and water in a 1-quart saucepan. Sprinkle gelatin over top. Simmer, stirring constantly, until the gelatin dissolves. Remove from the heat. Stir in the white wine. Pour gelatin mixture into a 4-cup mold. Insert a bowl, one size smaller, into the mold. Refrigerate for 1 hour or until set. Remove the smaller bowl.

Insert Steel Blade

Place onion in the Work Bowl; mince.

Heat the butter in a 12-inch frying pan. Add onion; sauté for 1 minute, stirring occasionally. Add livers, salt, nutmeg, and cinnamon; sauté until the liver is no longer red. Remove from heat and cool.

Insert Steel Blade

Place liver mixture in the Work Bowl; pulse 4 times; then process nonstop until puréed.

Pour mixture into aspic mold. Cover and chill for 6 hours. To unmold, carefully run a knife around the bowl to loosen. Cover the bottom of bowl with a hot towel for 5 seconds. Invert onto a serving platter. Serve with thin slices of bread or crackers.

Tangy Sausage and Veal Paté

Makes 8 servings.

- ½ pound bacon, blanched
- 4 sprigs parsley, rinsed and patted dry
- 2 slices dry white bread, each slice torn into 6 pieces
- ½ cup milk
- 3 cloves garlic
- 1 medium onion, quartered, or 4 shallots
- 1¼ pounds veal, cut into ¾-inch pieces
- ¾ pound pork, cut into ¾-inch pieces
- 1¼ pounds mildly spiced sausage with casing removed, cut into ¾-inch pieces
- 2 eggs, lightly beaten
- ⅓ cup Cognac
- ½ teaspoon crushed thyme
- 4 large bay leaves

Line a 9 x 5-inch loaf pan with bacon strips; reserve 2 strips bacon for topping.

Insert Steel Blade

Place parsley in the Work Bowl; mince; set aside. Add bread; process into crumbs. Place bread crumbs in a mixing bowl. Add milk to bread crumbs; mix well; set aside.

With the processor running, drop garlic through the Feed Tube; mince. Leave garlic in Work Bowl. Add onion; mince. Add onion and garlic to bread crumbs.

Add veal to the Work Bowl; mince. Add to mixing bowl.

Add pork to the Work Bowl; mince. Add to mixing bowl; mix well.

Add sausage to the Work Bowl; mince. Add to mixing bowl; mix well.

Add eggs, Cognac, and thyme to mixing bowl; mix well. Pack paté into the prepared loaf pan. Arrange bay leaves on top. Cover with remaining bacon strips. Cover with aluminum foil. Place loaf pan in a larger pan. Fill outside pan with 2 inches of hot water.

Preheat oven to 325°. Bake paté for 2 hours, until juices are clear; drain. Cool to room temperature. Chill overnight. Remove bay leaves. Unmold onto a serving platter. Slice thinly and serve with crisp French bread.

Soups

Spring Cream of Asparagus Soup

Makes 6 servings.

- ¾ pound fresh asparagus, cut into 1-inch pieces and steamed until tender
- 1 medium onion, quartered
- 5 tablespoons butter
- 1 teaspoon salt
- ½ teaspoon white pepper
- 6 cups beef bouillon
- 2 cups light cream
  Ground nutmeg

Insert Steel Blade

Place half of the asparagus in the Work Bowl; purée; set aside. Process remaining asparagus. Add onion to the Work Bowl; mince; set aside.

Melt butter in a 4-quart stockpot. Add onion and sauté for 2 minutes, stirring occasionally. Add asparagus, salt, and pepper; mix well. Stir in beef bouillon. Simmer for 20 minutes. Stir in cream. Simmer just to heat through. Pour into 6 soup bowls. Sprinkle nutmeg over soup.

Mulligatawny Soup

Makes 8 to 10 servings.

- 2 cloves garlic
- 1 medium onion, quartered
- 1 large apple, peeled, cored, and cut into 1-inch pieces
- 1½ cups cooked turkey, boned, and cut into 1-inch pieces
- 4 ribs celery, trimmed and cut into 4-inch lengths
- 1 medium carrot, pared and cut into 1-inch chunks
- 5 tablespoons butter
- 6 cups chicken bouillon
- 1 teaspoon curry powder
- ½ teaspoon salt
- ¼ cup cornstarch
- ¼ cup water
- 1 cup half-and-half

Insert Steel Blade

With the processor running, drop the garlic through the Feed Tube; mince 5 seconds; set aside. Add onion to the Work Bowl; mince 5 seconds; set aside. Add apple to the Work Bowl; chop roughly; set aside. Add turkey to the Work Bowl; chop roughly; set aside.

Insert Slicing Disc

Fit celery vertically into the Feed Tube; slice with light pressure; set aside.

Insert Grating Disc

Stand carrot vertically in the Feed Tube; grate; set aside.

Melt butter in a 4-quart stockpot. Sauté garlic, onion, and celery for 3 minutes, stirring occasionally. Add apple, turkey, and carrot; sauté for 1 minute. Add bouillon, curry powder, and salt. Simmer for 30 minutes. Combine cornstarch and water; stir into soup. Simmer until soup thickens, stirring constantly. Add cream; simmer just until heated through.

Vichyssoise

Makes 8 servings.

- 4 large leeks, white part only, cleaned
- 1 large onion, quartered
- 5 tablespoons butter
- 6 medium potatoes, peeled and quartered
- 5 cups chicken bouillon
- 1½ cups heavy cream, chilled and whipped
- ½ teaspoon salt
- ¼ teaspoon white pepper
- ¼ cup chives, cut into 1-inch pieces, optional

Insert Slicing Disc

Fit leeks vertically into the Feed Tube; slice; set aside. Fit onion into the Feed Tube; slice with light pressure; set aside.

Melt butter in a 3- to 4-quart saucepan. Add leeks and onion; sauté for 3 minutes or until tender, stirring occasionally.

Insert Slicing Disc

Fit potatoes into the Feed Tube; slice. Add potatoes and chicken bouillon to the pan.

Bring to a boil; reduce heat and simmer for 30 minutes or until vegetables are tender. Cool to room temperature.

Insert Steel Blade

Place 2½ cups of the vegetables in the Work Bowl; purée 10 to 15 seconds. Pour vegetables into a bowl. Repeat until all of the vegetables are puréed. Stir in cream.

Refrigerate until chilled. Sprinkle with salt and pepper. Pour into individual soup bowls.

Insert Steel Blade

Place chives in the Work Bowl; mince 5 seconds. Garnish soup with minced chives.

Gazpacho

Makes 8 to 10 servings.

- 3 cloves garlic
- 1 small onion, cut in half
- 2 large tomatoes, peeled and quartered
- 1 cucumber, peeled, cut in half lengthwise, and seeded
- ½ cup pitted black olives
- 1 green pepper, seeded and cut into 1-inch chunks
- ½ teaspoon Worcestershire sauce
- ½ teaspoon lemon juice
- 1 quart tomato juice
- 2 cups seasoned croutons

Insert Steel Blade

With the processor running, drop the garlic and onion through the Feed Tube; mince. Place garlic and onion in a large mixing bowl.

Add tomatoes to the Work Bowl; purée. Add to mixing bowl.

Insert Slicing Disc

Stand cucumber halves vertically in the Feed Tube; slice with light pressure. Add to the soup. Arrange olives randomly in the Feed Tube; slice with light pressure. Add to the soup.

Insert Steel Blade

Place green pepper in the Work Bowl; chop. Add to soup.

Stir in Worcestershire sauce, lemon juice, and tomato juice. Refrigerate until thoroughly chilled. Garnish with seasoned croutons.

Oxtail Soup

(Best when made at least 1 day in advance.)
Makes 8 servings.

- 3 sprigs parsley, rinsed and patted dry
- 4 tomatoes, peeled and quartered
- 1 large onion, quartered
- 3 ribs celery, trimmed and cut into 4-inch lengths
- 4 carrots, pared and cut into 1-inch chunks
- 5 tablespoons butter
- 2½ pounds oxtails
- 6 cups beef bouillon
- 2 cups water
- ½ teaspoon salt
- ½ teaspoon crushed thyme
- ½ teaspoon crushed sweet basil
- 3 bay leaves
- 3 cups cooked rice

Insert Steel Blade

Place parsley in the Work Bowl; mince; set aside. Add 2 tomatoes; chop roughly; set aside. Process remaining 2 tomatoes; set aside.

Insert Slicing Disc

Fit onion into the Feed Tube; slice with light pressure; set aside. Fit celery vertically into the Feed Tube; slice with light pressure; set aside. Arrange carrots vertically in the Feed Tube; slice; set aside.

Melt butter in a 4-quart stockpot. Sauté oxtails and onions until oxtails are lightly browned. Add parsley, tomatoes, celery, carrots, bouillon, water, salt, thyme, basil, and bay leaves; mix well. Simmer, uncovered, for 1 hour. Cool soup to room temperature. Refrigerate until thoroughly chilled. Skim fat. Reheat soup. Adjust seasonings; remove bay leaves. Serve in bowls over rice.

Bouillabaisse

Makes 10 to 12 servings.

- 5 sprigs parsley, rinsed and patted dry
- 2 cloves garlic
- 4 large tomatoes, peeled and quartered
- 2 ribs celery, trimmed and cut into 4-inch lengths
- 2 large leeks, white part only, cleaned and cut into 4-inch lengths
- ½ pound mushrooms, trimmed
- 1 large onion, quartered
- 3 tablespoons olive oil
- 3 tablespoons butter
- 2 cups clam juice
- 4 cups tomato juice
- 1 teaspoon salt
- ½ teaspoon black pepper
- ¼ teaspoon saffron, optional
- 5 large bay leaves
- 3 pounds firm fish filets, such as red snapper, sea bass, or scrod, cut into 2-inch pieces
- 12 large shrimp, peeled, deveined, leaving head and tail intact
- 1 pound scallops
- 12 mussels in shells, scrubbed
- 1 pound king crab legs, split and cut into 3-inch pieces (Ask fishmonger to help.)

Insert Steel Blade

Place parsley in the Work Bowl; mince 10 to 12 seconds. Set aside for garnish. Wipe Bowl dry with a damp cloth.

With the processor running, drop the garlic

through the Feed Tube; mince 5 seconds; set aside. Add half of the tomatoes; chop 2 to 4 seconds; set aside. Process remaining tomatoes.

Insert Slicing Disc

Stand celery vertically in the Feed Tube; slice with light pressure; set aside. Add leeks; slice; set aside. Fit mushrooms randomly into the Feed Tube; slice with light pressure; set aside. Place onion in the Feed Tube; slice; set aside.

Heat oil and butter in a 4- to 5-quart stockpot. Add garlic, celery, leeks, onion; sauté for 3 minutes, stirring occasionally. Add tomatoes, mushrooms, clam juice, tomato juice, salt, pepper, saffron, and bay leaves; simmer 5 minutes. Add fish; simmer for 10 minutes. Add shrimp, scallops, mussels, and crab leg pieces. Simmer for 10 minutes or until the fish is tender. Add more clam or tomato juice, if necessary. Adjust seasonings; discard bay leaves.

To serve

Sliced dry French bread

Place a slice of bread in each soup bowl. Spoon some of the fish over the bread. Ladle soup over the fish. Sprinkle parsley on top.

Butternut Bisque

Makes 8 servings.

    3 tart cooking apples, such as Granny Smith, peeled, cored, and quartered
    1 large onion, quartered
    2 pounds butternut squash, peeled, seeded, and cut into 2-inch chunks
    4 cups chicken bouillon
    ½ teaspoon crushed marjoram
    ½ teaspoon salt
    ¼ teaspoon white pepper
    2 cups heavy cream, chilled and beaten until soft peaks form
    2 large, sweet apples, cored, and quartered

Insert Slicing Disc

Fit apple wedges horizontally into the Feed Tube; slice. Place in a 3-quart saucepan.

Insert Steel Blade

Place onion in the Work Bowl; chop for 5 seconds.

Add onion, squash, bouillon, marjoram, salt, and pepper to the saucepan. Cover and simmer

for 45 minutes or until the squash is tender.

Insert Steel Blade

Add half of the squash mixture to the Work Bowl; purée. Remove mixture to a large mixing bowl. Process remaining squash.

Add puréed squash to the mixing bowl; blend thoroughly. Fold in cream.

Insert Slicing Disc

Fit apples horizontally into the Feed Tube; slice with light pressure.

Pour soup into individual bowls. Garnish with sliced apples. Serve chilled.

Cream of Broccoli Soup

Makes 8 servings.

    2 cloves garlic
    1 pound broccoli, cleaned, cut into 1-inch pieces, cooked, and drained
    6 ounces Swiss cheese, cut into ½-inch pieces and brought to room temperature
    1 medium onion, quartered
    4 tablespoons butter
    6 cups chicken bouillon
    ½ teaspoon salt
    ¼ teaspoon black pepper
    2 cups half-and-half
    ¼ cup cornstarch
    ¼ cup water

Insert Steel Blade

With the machine running, drop the garlic through the Feed Tube; mince 5 seconds; set aside. Place half of the broccoli in the Work Bowl; purée; set aside. Process remaining broccoli; set aside.

With the machine running, drop the cheese through the Feed Tube; process until fine; set aside.

Insert Slicing Disc

Fit onion into the Feed Tube; slice with light pressure.

Melt butter in a 3-quart saucepan. Add garlic and onion; sauté for 2 minutes, stirring occasionally. Add broccoli, cheese, bouillon, salt, pepper, and half-and-half. Simmer until the cheese melts.

Combine cornstarch and water; mix into a paste. Stir cornstarch mixture into the soup; stir until soup thickens.

Salads

Waldorf Salad

Makes 6 servings.

- ¾ cup walnut halves
- 3 large, firm apples, peeled, cored, and quartered
- 1 tablespoon lemon juice
- 5 ribs celery, trimmed and cut into 4-inch lengths
- 6 large lettuce leaves
- 1½ cups cottage cheese
- 1 cup Mayonnaise (Recipe on page 27)
- 1 cup golden raisins

Insert Steel Blade

Place walnuts in the Work Bowl; chop roughly; set aside.

Insert Slicing Disc

Fit apples into the Feed Tube; slice; set aside. Sprinkle lemon juice over apples.

Fit celery vertically into the Feed Tube; slice with light pressure; set aside.

Arrange lettuce on 6 plates. Place ¼ cup cottage cheese in the middle of each. Combine walnuts, apples, celery, and Mayonnaise. Spoon mixture over lettuce. Sprinkle with raisins.

Coleslaw

Makes 8 servings.

- 1 small head cabbage, cored and cut into Feed Tube-size pieces
- 1 medium onion, cut in half
- 1 medium carrot, peeled, cut into 1-inch chunks
- ½ teaspoon salt
- 3 tablespoons granulated sugar
- ½ teaspoon garlic powder
- ¼ cup wine vinegar
- ¼ teaspoon white pepper
- ¾ cup Mayonnaise (Recipe on page 27)

Insert Slicing Disc

Fit cabbage wedges into the Feed Tube; slice with light pressure. Place cabbage in a large bowl. Process remaining cabbage. Fit onion into the Feed Tube; slice with light pressure. Add onion to cabbage; toss lightly.

Insert Grating Disc

Fit carrot into the Feed Tube; grate. Add carrot to cabbage; mix lightly.

Sprinkle salt, sugar, garlic powder, vinegar and pepper over coleslaw; mix well. Stir in Mayonnaise. Chill thoroughly before serving.

European Cucumber Salad

Makes 10 servings.

- 6 large cucumbers, peeled, vertically sliced, and seeded
- 3 large onions, quartered
- ¼ cup red wine vinegar
- ⅓ cup granulated sugar
- ½ teaspoon salt
- ¼ teaspoon white pepper
- 1 cup sour cream

Insert Slicing Disc

Fit cucumbers vertically into the Feed Tube; slice with light pressure. Empty Work Bowl when fill level is reached; place cucumbers in a deep glass bowl. Fit onions into the Feed Tube; slice.

Combine onions and cucumbers. Sprinkle vinegar, sugar, salt, and pepper over salad; mix well. Chill until ready to serve. Serve in sauce dishes garnished with sour cream.

Fruit Salad

Makes 10 servings.

- ½ medium head iceberg lettuce, broken into bite-size pieces
- 1 large honeydew melon, chilled, seeded, and cut into Feed Tube-size pieces
- 4 large bananas
- 1 large avocado, peeled and pit removed
- 3 large oranges, halved and chilled
- 1 mango, seeded and cut into 1-inch pieces
- 1 quart strawberries, hulled
- 5 tablespoons lime juice

Arrange lettuce on a serving tray or 10 individual fruit plates.

Insert Slicing Disc

Fit the melon into the Feed Tube; slice with light pressure. Arrange on top of lettuce. Slice bananas with light pressure; arrange over the melon. Slice avocado; arrange on lettuce. Fit oranges into the bottom of the Feed Tube; slice with medium-heavy pressure. Arrange on the lettuce.

Sprinkle mango and strawberries over fruit. Drizzle lime juice over fruit. Cover with plastic wrap and refrigerate until ready to serve. Serve with Lime Dressing. (Recipe on page 27.)

Fruit Salad
Lime Dressing, 27

Mushroom Salad

Makes 6 servings.

   6 bunches bibb lettuce, separated
   ¾ pound mushrooms, cleaned and trimmed
   1 medium red onion, halved

Arrange lettuce on 6 chilled salad plates.

Insert Slicing Disc

Fit mushrooms alternately into the Feed Tube; slice with firm pressure; sprinkle over lettuce. Add onion to the Feed Tube; slice; sprinkle over mushrooms. Prepare Dressing. Sprinkle Dressing over salad.

Dressing

   1 small onion, quartered
   ½ cup vegetable oil
   ¼ cup red wine vinegar
   2 teaspoons granulated sugar
   1 teaspoon dry mustard
   ½ teaspoon salt
   ½ teaspoon black pepper

Insert Steel Blade

With the processor running, drop the onion through the Feed Tube; mince. Add remaining ingredients; combine.

Caesar Salad

Makes 6 servings.

   4 eggs
   4 cloves garlic
   1 medium onion, quartered
   1 2-ounce can anchovies, include oil
   ¼ teaspoon white pepper
   ½ cup vegetable oil
   1 large bunch romaine lettuce
   3 slices white bread, toasted and broken into
     6 pieces each
   6 ounces Parmesan cheese, room temperature,
     cut into ½-inch pieces

Bring a small saucepan of water to a boil; carefully place eggs in water; boil for 1 minute. Remove and set aside.

Insert Steel Blade

With the processor running, drop the garlic through the Feed Tube; mince. Push the garlic down the sides of the Work Bowl with a rubber spatula. Leave garlic in Work Bowl. Add onion, anchovies, pepper, and eggs; process just to combine. With the processor running, pour oil through the Feed Tube. Cover and refrigerate until ready to serve.

Divide lettuce among 6 chilled salad plates. Drizzle dressing over lettuce.

Insert Steel Blade

Add bread to Work Bowl; chop roughly. Sprinkle over salad. With the machine running, drop the cheese through the Feed Tube; process until fine. Sprinkle cheese over salad.

Salad Nicoise

Makes 6 to 8 servings.

   1 medium head iceberg lettuce, cut into Feed
     Tube-size pieces
   3 large tomatoes, peeled and halved
   1 cucumber, peeled, cut vertically in half
     and seeded
   1 medium onion, cut in half
   3 large potatoes, peeled, boiled, cooled,
     and quartered
   1 large green pepper, cut vertically in half
     and seeded
   1 cup whole, pitted ripe olives
   1 2-ounce can anchovies, drained
   2 6½-ounce cans tuna, drained and flaked
   1 medium lemon, ends trimmed

Insert Slicing Disc

Fit lettuce into the Feed Tube; slice with light pressure. Slice remaining lettuce. Remove lettuce from the Work Bowl when fill level is reached. Arrange lettuce on a serving platter.

Fit tomatoes into the Feed Tube; slice with light pressure. Arrange over lettuce. Slice remaining tomatoes.

Fit cucumber vertically into the Feed Tube; slice with light pressure. Arrange cucumber on the platter.

Fit onion in place; slice with light pressure. Arrange on lettuce.

Fit the potatoes into the Feed Tube; slice. Slice remaining potatoes. Arrange potatoes on the salad.

Curl pepper into the bottom of the Feed Tube; slice. Arrange pepper over salad.

Place the olives randomly in the Feed Tube; slice with light pressure. Sprinkle olives over salad.

Decoratively arrange anchovies over salad.

Place chunks of tuna between anchovies. Refrigerate until ready to serve.

Fit lemon into the Feed Tube; slice; set aside for garnish.

Prepare Dressing. Sprinkle over salad.

Dressing

  3 cloves garlic
  3 tablespoons wine vinegar
  ½ teaspoon dry mustard
  ½ teaspoon salt
  ¼ teaspoon black pepper
  3 tablespoons vegetable oil
  3 tablespoons olive oil

Insert Steel Blade

With the processor running, drop the garlic through the Feed Tube; mince. Add remaining ingredients; process until combined.

Spinach Salad

Makes 8 servings.

10 slices bacon, fried and crumbled; reserve drippings
  3 slices white bread, crusts removed, each torn into 6 pieces
  4 hard-cooked eggs, peeled
  1 large red onion, quartered
  1 pound spinach, cleaned and patted dry
  ¼ cup cider vinegar
  1 tablespoon granulated sugar
  1 teaspoon dry mustard
  ½ teaspoon salt
  ¼ teaspoon black pepper

Heat 3 tablespoons of the bacon drippings. Add bread and fry until drippings are absorbed and bread is crisp. Set aside.

Insert Steel Blade

Place bread in Work Bowl; chop roughly; set aside. Add eggs to Work Bowl; chop until fine; set aside.

Insert Slicing Disc

Fit onion into the Feed Tube; slice with light pressure; set aside.

Tear spinach into bite-size pieces. Place in a large salad bowl. Add bacon, bread, eggs, and onion; toss lightly.

Add ¼ cup of the warm bacon drippings.

Insert Plastic Blade

Place drippings, cider vinegar, sugar, mustard, salt, and pepper in the Work Bowl; combine. Sprinkle dressing over spinach salad; toss.

Cold Rice Salad

Makes 8 servings.

  3 cups cold cooked rice
  1 medium onion, quartered
  1 cup walnut halves
1½ cups cooked ham, cut into ½-inch cubes
  6 ounces Cheddar cheese, chilled and cut into Feed Tube-size pieces
  1 carrot, peeled and cut into 1-inch chunks

Place rice in a salad bowl.

Insert Steel Blade

Place onion in the Work Bowl; mince. Stir into rice. Place walnuts in the Work Bowl; chop. Stir into rice. Add ham; chop roughly. Stir into salad.

Insert Slicing Disc

Fit cheese into the Feed Tube; slice. Stir into rice.

Insert Grating Disc

Fit carrot into the Feed Tube; grate. Stir into rice.

Prepare Dressing. Sprinkle over salad. Chill until ready to serve.

Dressing

  ¼ cup vegetable oil
  ⅓ cup wine vinegar
  1 tablespoon granulated sugar

Insert Plastic Blade

Add oil, vinegar, and sugar to the Work Bowl; process until combined.

Cucumber and Onion Salad

Makes 4 servings.

  1 small cucumber
  1 small onion
  ¼ cup mayonnaise
  ½ teaspoon dillweed
  ½ teaspoon lemon juice
  ¼ teaspoon honey

Insert Slicing Disc

Stand cucumber in Feed Tube; slice; set aside. Insert onion in Feed Tube; slice; set aside. Empty Work Bowl as fill level is reached. Combine remaining ingredients in a small bowl. Drizzle over salad. Toss lightly before serving.

Dressings and Sauces

Walnut Oil Dressing

Makes ½ cup.

- 3 sprigs parsley, rinsed and patted dry
- 2 green onions, cut into 1-inch pieces; include tops
- 1 teaspoon dry mustard
- 1 tablespoon wine vinegar
- 3 tablespoons walnut oil
- 2 tablespoons salad oil
- ¼ teaspoon salt
- ¼ teaspoon black pepper

Insert Steel Blade

Add parsley and onions to the Work Bowl; mince. Leave onion mixture in the Work Bowl. Add remaining ingredients; process until combined. Refrigerate in a covered container until ready to serve. Serve over a green salad.

Yogurt and Blue Cheese Dressing

Makes 1½ cups.

- 2 cloves garlic
- 1 cup plain yogurt
- ½ cup Mayonnaise
- ½ cup blue cheese, crumbled into ½-inch chunks

Insert Steel Blade

With the processor running, drop the garlic through the Feed Tube; mince. Leave the garlic in the Bowl. Scrape sides of Work Bowl with a rubber spatula. Add yogurt and mayonnaise; combine. Add blue cheese; pulse for 2 seconds. Refrigerate in a covered container until ready to use. Serve over a green salad.

Poppy Seed Dressing

Makes ¾ cup.

- ¾ cup Mayonnaise
- 3 tablespoons granulated sugar
- 1½ tablespoons lemon juice
- 1 tablespoon poppy seeds

Insert Plastic Blade

Add mayonnaise, sugar, and lemon juice to the Work Bowl. Process until combined. Add poppy seeds; process until combined.

Refrigerate in a covered container until ready to use. Serve over fruit salad.

Mayonnaise

Makes 1½ cups.

- 3 extra large egg yolks
- 2 teaspoons lemon juice
- ½ teaspoon salt
- ¼ teaspoon white pepper
- ½ teaspoon dry mustard
- 1½ cups vegetable oil
- 2 tablespoons olive oil

Insert Steel Blade

Combine egg yolks, lemon juice, salt, pepper, and mustard in the Work Bowl; process 5 seconds. With the machine running, slowly pour oils in a thin, steady stream through the Feed Tube. Process until the mayonnaise is thick and creamy. Refrigerate in a covered container.

Green Mayonnaise

Makes 2¼ cups.

- ¾ cup parsley sprigs, rinsed and patted dry
- ¼ cup capers
- 3 extra large egg yolks
- 2 teaspoons wine vinegar
- ½ teaspoon salt
- ¼ teaspoon white pepper
- ½ teaspoon dry mustard
- 1½ cups vegetable oil
- 3 tablespoons olive oil

Insert Steel Blade

Add parsley and capers to the Work Bowl; mince 10 to 12 seconds. Leave parsley and capers in the Work Bowl. Add egg yolks, wine vinegar, salt, pepper, and mustard; process 5 seconds. With the machine running, slowly pour oils in a thin, steady stream through the Feed Tube; process until the mayonnaise is thick and creamy. Refrigerate in a covered container.

Lime Dressing

Makes 2⅔ cups.

- 1 cup Mayonnaise
- ⅓ cup lime juice
- ⅓ cup honey
- ½ cup heavy cream, chilled and whipped

Place Mayonnaise, lime juice, and honey in Work Bowl; process until combined. Add whipped cream; combine.

Hollandaise Sauce

Makes ¾ cup.

- 3 large egg yolks
- 1 tablespoon tarragon vinegar
- ¼ teaspoon salt
- ½ cup butter, melted

Insert Plastic Blade

Add egg yolks, vinegar, and salt to the Work Bowl. Process until thoroughly blended. With the machine running, pour the melted butter through the Feed Tube; process until the sauce is smooth and thick. If not used immediately, reheat sauce in a double boiler. Whisk until warm.

Mousseline Sauce

Makes 1¼ cups.

Mousseline sauce is a hollandaise sauce that has been lightened with whipped cream. Serve over chicken, fish or vegetables.

- ¾ cup Hollandaise Sauce (Recipe above)
- ½ cup heavy cream, chilled and whipped

Gently fold the whipped cream into the hollandaise.

Hot Chocolate Sauce

Makes 2½ cups.

- 6 ounces semisweet chocolate chips
- ½ cup heavy cream
- 6 tablespoons butter
- 1 cup granulated sugar
- 2 egg yolks
- 1½ teaspoons vanilla

Insert Steel Blade

Place chocolate in Work Bowl; process until chocolate is crushed. (Processor will be noisy.) Combine cream and butter in a saucepan. Heat until butter melts. Do *not* boil. With the processor running, pour cream through the Feed Tube and continue to process until chocolate is melted. Remove the cover. Add sugar, egg yolks, and vanilla. Process until blended, 4 seconds. Refrigerate in a covered container until ready to use.

Reheat in a double boiler.

Oil and Garlic Sauce

Makes 1½ cups.

- 3 cloves garlic
- 3 sprigs parsley, rinsed and patted dry
- 6 green onions, white part only, cut into 1½-inch pieces
- ½ cup butter
- 4 tablespoons olive oil
- ½ cup dry red wine

Insert Steel Blade

With the processor running, drop the garlic through the Feed Tube; mince; set aside. Place parsley in the Work Bowl; mince 10 seconds. Add onion; mince 5 seconds.

Heat butter and oil in a small saucepan. Add garlic, parsley, and onion; sauté for 1 minute, stirring occasionally. Stir in wine. Bring to a boil, remove from heat and serve over pasta.

Watercress Sauce for Fish

Makes 1¾ cups.

- 1 small onion, cut in half
- ½ cup watercress, rinsed and patted dry
- ¾ cup Mayonnaise (Recipe on page 27)
- ¾ cup sour cream
- ¼ teaspoon salt
- ¼ teaspoon white pepper

Insert Steel Blade

With the processor running, drop the onion through the Feed Tube; mince 5 seconds. Leave the onion in the Work Bowl. Add the watercress; mince 10 to 15 seconds. Add the mayonnaise, sour cream, salt, and pepper; process until creamy. Refrigerate in a covered container until ready to serve.

Tartar Sauce

Makes 1¼ cups.

- 1 medium onion, quartered
- 1 sweet pickle, cut in half
- 1 sprig parsley, rinsed and patted dry
- 1 cup Mayonnaise (Recipe on page 27)

Insert Steel Blade

Add onion to Work Bowl; mince 5 seconds. Add pickle and parsley; pulse 5 seconds. Add Mayonnaise; combine.

Place in a covered container and refrigerate until ready to use.

Barbecue Sauce

Makes 1¾ cups.

- 1 clove garlic
- 1 medium onion, quartered
- 1½ cups catsup
- 1 tablespoon vegetable oil
- 3 tablespoons wine vinegar
- 2 teaspoons Worcestershire sauce
- 3 tablespoons brown sugar
- ½ teaspoon Tabasco sauce

Insert Steel Blade

With the processor running, drop the garlic through the Feed Tube; mince about 5 seconds. Leave the garlic in the Work Bowl. Add the onion to the Work Bowl; mince about 5 seconds. Add remaining ingredients; process until sauce is smooth, about 4 seconds.

Refrigerate in a covered container until ready to serve.

To save clean-up time when making salad, mix the dressing ingredients in the bottom of the salad bowl. Add the remaining ingredients, except greens, and toss before serving.

Fall Corn Relish

Makes 1 quart.

- ¼ medium head cabbage, cored and cut into Feed Tube-size pieces
- 2 medium onions, quartered
- 4 ribs celery, trimmed and cut into 4-inch pieces
- 2 green peppers, halved and seeded
- 2½ cups raw corn, scraped from cob or canned corn, drained
- ½ cup granulated sugar
- ½ cup cider vinegar
- 2 teaspoons dry mustard
- 1 tablespoon salt
- ½ teaspoon turmeric

Insert Thin Slicing Disc or Regular Slicing Disc

Fit cabbage into Feed Tube; slice; place in a 4-quart saucepan. Slice onions with light pressure. Add to saucepan. Fit the celery vertically into the Feed Tube; slice with light pressure. Add celery to the saucepan. Curl the peppers into the bottom of the Feed Tube; slice with light pressure. Add to the saucepan. Add remaining ingredients. Cook over medium heat for 40 minutes, stirring occasionally. Cool.

Seafood Sauce

Makes 2¼ cups.

- 4 sprigs parsley
- 2 sweet pickles, cut into ½-inch pieces
- 1 cup Mayonnaise (Recipe on page 27)
- 1 cup sour cream
- ½ teaspoon crushed sweet basil
- ¼ teaspoon salt

Insert Steel Blade

Place parsley in Work Bowl; process until minced, about 10 to 12 seconds. Add the pickles; process until chopped. Add remaining ingredients; process 4 seconds. Refrigerate in a covered container.

Apricot Chutney

Makes 1 quart.

- 1 clove garlic
- 1¾ cups dried apricots, washed, drained, and chilled
- 3 tablespoons candied ginger, cut into ½-inch pieces
- 1 small lemon, rind removed
- 1 large onion, quartered
- 1½ cups dark raisins
- 1¾ cups packed light brown sugar
- ¾ cup wine vinegar
- 2 teaspoons Tabasco sauce
- ¾ cup tomato juice
- ½ teaspoon salt
- ¾ teaspoon ground cinnamon
- ½ teaspoon ground cloves
- ¼ teaspoon allspice

Insert Steel Blade

With the processor running, drop the garlic through the Feed Tube; mince 5 seconds. Place in a heavy, 2-quart saucepan.

Place apricots in the Work Bowl; process until coarsely chopped. Add apricots to garlic.

With the processor running, drop the ginger through the Feed Tube; chop. Add ginger to the saucepan.

Insert Slicing Disc

Place lemon in the bottom of the Feed Tube; slice with medium-heavy pressure. Add to saucepan. Fit onion into the Feed Tube; slice with light pressure. Add onion and remaining ingredients to the saucepan. Simmer for 30 minutes, stirring occasionally. Cool. Refrigerate in a covered container.

Puréed Turnips and Pears

Makes 6 to 8 servings.

- 2½ pounds white turnips, peeled and quartered
- 6 tablespoons butter
- 1 16-ounce can pears, drained
- ¼ teaspoon salt
- ¼ teaspoon ground nutmeg

Place turnips in a 2-quart saucepan. Cover with water and cook over medium heat until turnips are tender. Drain and cool.

Insert Steel Blade

Place ⅓ of the turnips, 2 tablespoons of the butter, and ⅓ of the pears in the Work Bowl; purée. Remove to a large mixing bowl. Purée remaining turnips, butter, and pears in thirds.

Combine all ingredients, including spices. Mound into a buttered 9-inch baking dish. Bake at 375° for 20 minutes.

Fresh from the Garden Casserole

Makes 6 to 8 servings.

- 3 small carrots, peeled and cut into 1-inch lengths
- ½ pound green beans, trimmed to fit Feed Tube
- 1 small yellow squash, cut in 2-inch pieces
- 1 small zucchini, cut in 2-inch pieces
- ½ head cauliflower, broken into flowerets
- 1 cup chicken bouillon
- 1 teaspoon salt
- ½ teaspoon white pepper
- 1 clove garlic
- 4 tablespoons butter

Insert Slicing Disc

Place carrots in Feed Tube; slice; set aside. Place beans horizontally in the Feed Tube; slice; set aside. Place squash in Feed Tube; slice; set aside. Place zucchini in Feed Tube; slice; set aside.

Place all vegetables in a buttered 2-quart casserole.

Heat bouillon in a small saucepan. Add salt and pepper.

With the processor running, drop the garlic down the Feed Tube. Add to bouillon. Pour over vegetables. Dot top with butter.

Cover and bake in a 350° oven for 30 minutes or until all vegetables are tender.

Glazed Carrots

Makes 8 to 10 servings.

- 1½ pounds carrots, trimmed and cut into Feed Tube-size pieces
- 2 teaspoons salt
- 1 cup sliced almonds
- 1 medium orange, cut in half and seeded
- 4 tablespoons butter
- 2 tablespoons cornstarch
- 2 tablespoons brown sugar
- ½ teaspoon salt
- ¼ teaspoon ground nutmeg
- ⅓ cup orange juice

Insert Slicing Disc

Fit carrots vertically into the Feed Tube; slice. Remove carrots to a 4-quart saucepan. Cover with water. Add salt. Simmer 10 minutes or until carrots are tender; drain.

Insert Steel Blade

Add almonds to Work Bowl; chop; set aside. Processor will be noisy. Fit orange into the bottom of the Feed Tube; slice; set aside.

Place carrots in a heated vegetable dish. Melt butter in a small saucepan. Whisk in cornstarch. Add brown sugar, salt, nutmeg, and orange juice. Simmer until mixture thickens, stirring constantly. Add orange slices. Pour mixture over carrots. Sprinkle almonds over carrots.

Deep-Fried Potato Slices

Makes 4 servings.

- 4 medium-small potatoes, peeled and cut to fit Feed Tube
- 2 cups vegetable oil
- ½ teaspoon salt

Insert Slicing Disc

Fit potatoes into the Feed Tube; slice. Place potatoes in a large mixing bowl. Slice remaining potatoes.

Cover potatoes with cold water. Let stand for 30 minutes; change water once. Drain potatoes. Pat dry with paper toweling. Heat oil to 375° in a 3-quart saucepan or small frying pan. Slide a third of the potatoes into the hot oil. Deep fry until golden brown on both sides, stirring frequently. Drain on paper toweling. Sprinkle on salt. Serve hot. Potatoes can be kept warm in a 350° oven until ready to serve.

French-Fried Onion Rings
Makes 8 servings.

    6 small Feed Tube-size onions, peeled
    1 cup unbleached all-purpose flour
    ½ teaspoon salt
    ½ cup milk
    1 tablespoon vegetable oil
    1 egg white, lightly beaten
    5 tablespoons water
    2 cups vegetable oil
    1 tablespoon salt

Insert Slicing Disc
Place onions in the Feed Tube; slice with light pressure. Separate rings and set aside.

Insert Steel Blade
Add flour, salt, milk, oil, egg white, and water to the Work Bowl; pulse just until combined. Set mixture aside in a large bowl. Let stand 15 minutes at room temperature; stir.

Heat oil to 375° in an 8- to 10-inch frying pan. Dip onion rings into the batter. Slide rings into the hot oil. Fry until golden brown on both sides; turn once. Drain on paper toweling. Sprinkle on salt.

Creamy Green Beans
Makes 8 servings.

    2 pounds green beans, trimmed to fit horizontally
       into the Feed Tube
    2 teaspoons salt
    2 sprigs parsley, rinsed and patted dry
    3 cloves garlic
    5 tablespoons butter
    ½ cup half-and-half

Insert Slicing Disc
Arrange green beans horizontally in the Feed Tube; slice with light pressure; set aside.

Place green beans in a large saucepan. Sprinkle on salt. Cover with water. Simmer for 10 minutes; drain.

Insert Steel Blade
Add parsley to the Work Bowl; mince; set aside. With the processor running, drop the garlic through the Feed Tube; mince; set aside.

Melt butter in a large saucepan. Add garlic and sauté for 30 seconds. Add green beans; mix well. Stir in half-and-half. Simmer for 1 minute. Place beans in a warm serving bowl. Sprinkle on minced parsley.

Harvard Beets
Makes 8 servings.

    6 large fresh beets, peeled and quartered
    1 large onion, quartered
    ⅓ cup granulated sugar
    ¼ cup cornstarch
    2 tablespoons butter
    ⅓ cup wine vinegar
    ¾ cup water

Insert Slicing Disc
Fit beets into the Feed Tube; slice. Place beets in a 3-quart saucepan. Cover with water. Simmer until tender; drain.

Place onion in the Feed Tube; slice with light pressure. Add onion to beets; set aside.

Combine sugar, cornstarch, butter, vinegar, and water in a small bowl; mix well. Add to beets. Bring mixture to a boil. Reduce heat and simmer until the mixture thickens, stirring often. Place beets in a serving dish.

Layered Vegetables
Makes 12 servings.

    4 ribs celery, trimmed and cut into 4-inch lengths
    5 medium onions, cut in half
    3 red bell peppers, cut vertically in half and seeded
    8 medium plum tomatoes
    ½ pound string beans, trimmed to fit Feed Tube
    1 5¼-ounce can pitted black olives, drained
  1½ cups Green Mayonnaise (Recipe on page 27)

Insert Slicing Disc
Fit celery vertically into the Feed Tube; slice with light pressure. Arrange celery in a 2-quart soufflé dish or salad bowl.

Fit the onions into the Feed Tube; slice with light pressure. Scatter onions over the celery. Curl peppers into the bottom of the Feed Tube; slice. Arrange pepper slices over onions. Place tomatoes top-side up in the Feed Tube; slice. Arrange tomatoes over the peppers.

Arrange the beans horizontally in the Feed Tube; slice. Sprinkle beans over tomatoes. Carefully stand olives on top of the Slicing Disc under the Feed Tube. Attach cover. Press Pusher onto olives; slice. Sprinkle olives over the beans. Spread mayonnaise over the top of the vegetables. Refrigerate until ready to serve.

Caponata

Makes 3 cups.

- 4 sprigs parsley, rinsed and patted dry
- 3 cloves garlic
- 2 medium onions, quartered
- 3 tomatoes, peeled and quartered
- ¾ cup pimiento-stuffed olives
- 6 ribs celery, trimmed and cut into 4-inch lengths
- 1 medium eggplant, quartered vertically
- ⅓ cup olive oil
- ⅓ cup wine vinegar
- 1 teaspoon honey
- ½ cup water
- 2 tablespoons capers
- ½ teaspoon salt
- ¼ teaspoon black pepper

Insert Steel Blade

Place parsley in the Work Bowl; mince; set aside. With the processor running, drop the garlic through the Feed Tube; mince. Add the onions; mince; set aside. Add tomatoes; chop roughly; set aside. Add olives to the Work Bowl; chop; set aside.

Insert Slicing Disc

Fit celery vertically into the Feed Tube; slice with light pressure; set aside. Slice eggplant with light pressure; set aside.

Heat olive oil in a 2-quart saucepan. Add garlic, onion, and celery; sauté for 3 minutes. Push vegetables to sides of the pan.

Add eggplant; sauté until tender.

Add remaining ingredients; simmer for 20 minutes, stirring occasionally. Cool. Place in a covered container and refrigerate overnight. Serve with crudités and buttered toast triangles.

Potato Pancakes

Makes 6 servings.

- 4 large potatoes, peeled and quartered to fit Feed Tube
- 1 medium onion, quartered
- 1 egg, lightly beaten
- ½ teaspoon salt
- ¼ teaspoon black pepper
- 3 tablespoons unbleached all-purpose flour
- 6 tablespoons vegetable oil

Insert Grating Disc

Fit potatoes into the Feed Tube; grate with medium pressure. Grate remaining potatoes. Place in a large mixing bowl.

Place onion in the Feed Tube; grate. Add onion to potato; mix lightly.

Insert Steel Blade

Add 1½ cups of the potato mixture to the Work Bowl; process until mixture resembles fine coleslaw. Process remaining potatoes. Place potatoes in a large mixing bowl.

Add egg, salt, pepper, and flour; mix well. Heat oil in a large frying pan. Slide potato mixture by tablespoonfuls into the hot oil. Fry, turning once, until crisp and golden brown on both sides. Serve hot. Potato pancakes can be reheated in a 350° oven for 15 minutes, covered with aluminum foil for soft pancakes and uncovered for crispy pancakes.
Serve with applesauce.

Spinach Timbales

Makes 6 servings.

- 2 cloves garlic
- 1 small onion, cut in half
- 1½ pounds fresh spinach, cooked and drained
- 1 medium lemon, ends removed, optional
- 6 tablespoons butter, melted
- 3 tablespoons unbleached all-purpose flour
- 1 cup milk
- 4 eggs, lightly beaten
- ½ teaspoon salt
- ¼ teaspoon ground nutmeg

Insert Steel Blade

With the processor running, drop the garlic and onion through the Feed Tube; mince; set aside. Add the spinach; purée; set aside.

Insert Slicing Disc

Fit lemon into the bottom of the Feed Tube; slice with medium pressure; remove seeds. Remove for garnish.

Preheat oven to 375°. Butter six timbale molds (available at gourmet shops) or custard cups with 3 tablespoons of the melted butter. Heat remaining butter in a saucepan. Add garlic and onion and sauté 3 to 4 minutes; drain any excess liquid. Stir in flour until it is absorbed. Add milk and eggs; stir until the mixture thickens. Blend in spinach, salt, and nutmeg. Pour spinach mixture into the prepared molds. Place molds in a baking pan. Add 1½ inches water. Bake for 20 minutes or until timbales are firm. Let stand at room temperature for 5 minutes. Unmold. Serve cold or hot.

Beef

Mild Goulash

Makes 5 to 6 servings.

- 2 cloves garlic
- 3 medium tomatoes, peeled and quartered
- 1 large onion, quartered
- 3 tablespoons vegetable oil
- 2 tablespoons butter
- 1¾ pounds chuck steak, cut into ½-inch cubes
- 1 tablespoon paprika
- ½ teaspoon salt
- 3 tablespoons catsup
- 1 cup sour cream

Insert Steel Blade

With the machine running, drop the garlic down the Feed Tube; mince; set aside.

Add tomatoes to the Work Bowl; chop; set aside.

Insert Slicing Disc

Fit onion into the Feed Tube; slice; set aside.

Heat oil and butter in a 4-quart saucepan. Add garlic and onion; sauté for 1 minute, stirring occasionally. Add cubed steak; sauté until browned. Add tomatoes, paprika, salt, and catsup; mix well. Cover and simmer for 50 minutes. Serve over buttered noodles. Garnish with sour cream.

Pepper Steak

Makes 4 to 5 servings.

- 3 tablespoons cornstarch
- ½ cup beef bouillon
- 3 tablespoons soy sauce
- 1½ pounds flank steak, partially frozen and cut against the grain into Feed Tube-size pieces
- 1 large onion, quartered
- 2 large green peppers, cut in half and seeded
- 4 ribs celery, trimmed and cut into 4-inch lengths
- 2 cloves garlic
- 4 tablespoons peanut oil
- ½ teaspoon ground ginger
- ½ teaspoon salt
- ¼ teaspoon black pepper

Combine the first 3 ingredients.

Insert Wide or Regular Slicing Disc

Fit pieces of flank steak into the Feed Tube against the grain; slice with firm pressure. Empty Work Bowl when half filled. Slice remaining beef; set aside.

Fit onion into the Feed Tube; slice with light pressure; set aside.

Curl the pepper into the bottom of the Feed Tube; slice; set aside.

Fit the celery vertically into the Feed Tube; slice with light pressure; set aside.

Insert Steel Blade

With the processor running, drop the garlic down the Feed Tube; mince 5 seconds; set aside.

Heat the oil in a large frying pan. Add the garlic, onion, celery, and green pepper; sauté for 2 minutes, stirring occasionally. Add beef; stir-fry until the meat begins to lose its color. Sprinkle on ginger, salt, and pepper. Add bouillon mixture; stir until sauce begins to thicken. Serve over rice or noodles.

Sukiyaki

Makes 8 servings.

- 2 pounds flank steak, cut into 1 x 3-inch pieces, partially frozen
- 2 large onions, quartered
- 8 ribs celery, trimmed and cut into 4-inch lengths
- ½ pound mushrooms, trimmed
- ¼ cup peanut oil
- ½ teaspoon salt
- ¼ cup soy sauce
- 2 cups beef bouillon
- ¼ cup granulated sugar

Insert Slicing Blade

Fit beef into the Feed Tube; slice with firm pressure. (Machine might be noisy.) Set aside. Fit onion into the Feed Tube; slice with light pressure. Slice remaining onion; set aside. Fit celery vertically into the Feed Tube; slice with light pressure; set aside. Place mushrooms in the Feed Tube; slice with firm pressure; set aside. Arrange sliced meat and vegetables decoratively on a platter.

If cooking at the table, use an electric skillet or electric wok. Heat oil. Add onions and beef; stir-fry until beef is no longer red. Add vegetables, 1 group at a time; stir-fry until tender-crisp. Sprinkle on salt, soy sauce, bouillon, and sugar. Mix lightly. Serve over rice.

Bolognese Sauce

Makes 5 cups.

- 1 large onion, quartered
- 1 pound chuck steak, cut into ¾-inch pieces
- 2 28-ounce cans tomatoes, including juice
- 1 large carrot, pared and cut into 1-inch chunks
- 2 ribs celery, trimmed and cut into 4-inch lengths
- 2 tablespoons vegetable oil
- 2 tablespoons olive oil
- ⅓ cup dry red wine
- 1 teaspoon granulated sugar
- 1 6-ounce can tomato paste
- ¾ cup hot water
- ½ teaspoon salt

Insert Steel Blade

Place onion in the Work Bowl; mince 5 seconds; set aside. Add 1½ cups beef; chop 7 seconds. Chop remaining beef; set aside. Add half of the tomatoes; chop; set aside. Chop remaining tomatoes; set aside.

Insert Grating Disc

Place carrot vertically in the Feed Tube; grate with heavy pressure; set aside.

Insert Slicing Disc

Place celery vertically in the Feed Tube; slice; set aside.

Heat oils in a 3-quart saucepan. Add onion, carrot, and celery; sauté for 3 minutes, stirring occasionally. Add ground chuck steak; sauté until the meat is browned. Add tomatoes, juice, wine, sugar, tomato paste, water, and salt; blend thoroughly. Bring to a boil, reduce heat, and cover; simmer for 30 minutes. Remove cover. Simmer 15 minutes.

Spaghetti Sauce with Meat

Makes enough sauce for 8 servings.

- 2 cloves garlic
- 1 large onion, quartered
- 1 pound chuck steak, cut into ¾-inch pieces, gristle removed
- 2 16-ounce cans tomatoes, drained, reserve juice
- 3 tablespoons vegetable oil
- 1 6-ounce can tomato paste
- 2 cups water
- ½ teaspoon granulated sugar
- ½ teaspoon crushed oregano
- ½ teaspoon crushed sweet basil
- ½ teaspoon salt
- ¼ teaspoon black pepper

Insert Steel Blade

With the processor running, drop the garlic through the Feed Tube; mince 5 seconds. Add onion; mince; set aside. Add 2 cups of the beef; mince; set aside. Process remaining beef; set aside. Add half of the tomatoes; chop 4 seconds; set aside. Process remaining tomatoes.

Heat oil in a large saucepan. Add garlic and onion; sauté for 2 minutes. Add beef; sauté until lightly browned, stirring occasionally. Stir in remaining ingredients. Simmer, uncovered, for 45 minutes, stirring occasionally. Adjust seasonings.

Greek Meat and Macaroni Casserole

Makes 6 servings.

- 2 cloves garlic
- 2½ pounds lean chuck steak, cut into ¾-inch pieces
- 2 large tomatoes, peeled and quartered
- 1 large onion, quartered
- 3 tablespoons butter
- 1 tablespoon vegetable oil
- ½ teaspoon ground cinnamon
- ½ teaspoon Greek seasoning (Available at specialty food stores.)
- 1 teaspoon salt
- ½ teaspoon black pepper
- 6 tablespoons catsup
- ½ pound elbow macaroni, cooked according to package directions, drained, and kept warm
- 6 ounces Parmesan cheese, cut into ½-inch pieces and brought to room temperature

Insert Steel Blade

With the processor running, drop the garlic through the Feed Tube; mince; set aside. Add half of the beef; mince 7 seconds; remove to a large bowl. Mince remaining beef; set aside.

Add tomatoes to Work Bowl; chop; reserve.

Insert Slicing Disc

Fit onion into the Feed Tube; slice onion; set aside.

Heat butter and oil in a 12-inch frying pan. Sauté garlic and onion for 2 minutes, stirring occasionally. Add beef; brown, stirring occasionally. Sprinkle cinnamon, Greek seasoning, salt, and pepper over beef; mix lightly. Stir in tomatoes and catsup. Remove from heat.

Butter a 9-inch baking dish. Preheat oven to 350°. Combine beef mixture with macaroni in a large mixing bowl. Mound into prepared casserole.

Insert Steel Blade

With the Steel Blade in place and the processor running, drop the cheese through the Feed Tube; process until fine. Sprinkle cheese over casserole. Bake 45 minutes.

Stuffed Peppers

Makes 8 servings.

- 2 cloves garlic
- 1 large onion, quartered
- 1 pound chuck steak, cut into ¾-inch pieces
- 3 sprigs parsley, rinsed and patted dry
- 2 slices dry bread, each slice torn into 6 pieces
- 3 tablespoons vegetable oil
- ½ teaspoon salt
- 8 firm bell peppers, tops removed and seeded
- 2 cups Spaghetti Sauce with Meat, heated (Recipe on page 36)

Insert Steel Blade

With the machine running, drop the garlic through the Feed Tube; mince 5 seconds. Add the onion; mince; set aside. Add 2 cups of the beef; process until ground; set aside. Process remaining beef. Remove meat from the Work Bowl and set aside. Add parsley to Work Bowl; mince 10 seconds; set aside. Add the bread to the Work Bowl; process into crumbs; set aside.

Heat the oil in a large frying pan. Add garlic and onion; sauté for 2 minutes or until tender. Add beef, parsley, salt, and bread crumbs; sauté for 1 minute. Spoon beef mixture into peppers. Arrange peppers in an oiled baking dish. Cover with aluminum foil. Bake at 350° for 50 minutes. Remove foil. Bake peppers for 10 minutes. Place on a serving dish. Ladle Spaghetti Sauce over peppers.

Beef Hash

Makes 5 to 6 servings.

- 2 cups leftover beef, cut into ½-inch pieces
- 2½ cups boiled potatoes, cooled, and cut into ¾-inch pieces
- ½ teaspoon salt
- ¼ teaspoon black pepper
- ¼ teaspoon crushed thyme
- 1 8-ounce can tomato sauce
- 1 slice dry dark rye bread, torn into 6 pieces
- 2 tablespoons butter

Lightly butter a 9-inch baking dish.

Insert Steel Blade

Place beef in the Work Bowl; pulse 3 times; then process until coarsely chopped. Remove to a large mixing bowl.

Place half of the potatoes in the Work Bowl; chop roughly. Remove to the mixing bowl. Process remaining potatoes. Add to beef. Add salt, pepper, thyme, and tomato sauce to beef; blend thoroughly. Mound into the prepared dish.

Wipe out Work Bowl with a damp cloth. Add the bread to the Work Bowl; process to make crumbs, about 10 seconds. Sprinkle crumbs over meat mixture. Dot with butter. Bake in a preheated 375° oven for 15 minutes or until heated through.

Sweet and Sour Meat Loaf

Makes 4 to 6 servings.

- 2 pounds chuck steak, cut into 1-inch pieces
- ½ pound lean pork, cut into ¾-inch pieces
- 1 medium onion, cut in half
- 2 slices day-old white bread, cut into 6 pieces
- 2 extra large eggs, lightly beaten
- 1 14-ounce can tomato sauce
- ½ cup packed dark brown sugar
- ¼ cup wine vinegar
- ½ teaspoon prepared mustard

Insert Steel Blade

Add 1½ cups of the chuck steak to the Work Bowl; process for about 7 seconds or until ground. Process remaining chuck steak; set aside. Add pork to Work Bowl; chop. Place meats in a large mixing bowl. Place onion in the Work Bowl; chop. Add onion to meats; mix lightly. Place bread in Work Bowl; process into crumbs. Add crumbs to meat; mix well.

Combine eggs, tomato sauce, brown sugar, wine vinegar, and mustard in a medium bowl. Add 1 cup of the sauce to the meat mixture; mix thoroughly. Pack mixture into a buttered 9 x 5-inch loaf pan. Preheat oven to 350°. Pour one-third of the remaining sauce over the top of the meat loaf. Bake for 1 hour and 15 minutes. Remove from the oven; let stand for 5 minutes. Heat remaining sauce. Slice meat loaf and serve with sauce.

Pork, Veal, Lamb

Scandinavian Pork Roast with Apple Cream Sauce

Makes 4 to 6 servings.

    2   pounds pork tenderloin
    ½   cup heavy cream
    2   tablespoons sherry
    1   teaspoon white horseradish
    ¼   teaspoon salt
    4   large red Delicious apples, peeled,
        cored, and quartered
    2   medium onions, quartered
    5   tablespoons butter
    1   cup heavy cream
    ½   teaspoon ground nutmeg

Preheat oven to 400°. Place pork on a rack in a shallow roasting pan.

Insert Plastic Blade

Place cream, sherry, horseradish, and salt in the Work Bowl; process until mixed, about 3 seconds.

Drizzle sauce over pork. Bake 1 hour and 20 minutes or until pork is no longer pink.

Insert Slicing Disc

Fit apples randomly into the Feed Tube; slice with light pressure; set aside. Fit onions into the Feed Tube; slice with light pressure.

Heat butter in a large frying pan. Add apples and onions; sauté until soft, 2 to 4 minutes. Add cream and nutmeg; simmer for 3 minutes.

Slice pork. Place on a heated platter. Pour sauce over pork.

Pork Tenderloin with Olive Sauce

Makes 6 servings.

    ¼   cup butter
    2   tablespoons vegetable oil
    2   pounds pork tenderloin, cut into ½-inch slices
    1   large onion, quartered
    1   cup pitted, black olives
    ½   teaspoon dillweed
    2   cups sour cream

Heat butter and oil in a large frying pan. Brown the pork slices on each side until golden brown and tender; remove pork and reserve drippings.

Insert Slicing Disc

Fit the onion into the Feed Tube; slice with light pressure; set aside. Place olives randomly into the Feed Tube; slice; set aside.

Reheat drippings. Add onion and sauté for 2 minutes, stirring occasionally. Add olives and dillweed; blend thoroughly. Stir in sour cream. Return pork to pan. Spoon sauce over pork. Serve with hot rice or noodles.

Leg of Lamb with Parsley Crumb Crust

Makes 8 to 10 servings.

    3   cloves garlic
    1   5- to 6-pound leg of lamb, rinsed, dried,
        and trimmed of fat
    1   teaspoon salt
    ½   teaspoon black pepper
    2   tablespoons prepared mustard

Cut garlic cloves in half. Make six ½-inch slits on top of the lamb. Insert garlic slivers into the slits. Sprinkle salt and pepper over the lamb. Rub the mustard over the lamb. Preheat oven to 325°. Place lamb in a roasting pan. Place in oven. Prepare the Crumb Crust while the lamb is baking. After 1½ hours, remove lamb from oven. Press crumbs over all sides of the lamb. Return lamb to oven; bake for 30 minutes. Place on a heated serving platter. Slice lamb at the dinner table. Spoon crumbled Crust over sliced lamb.

Crumb Crust

    4   slices whole wheat bread, each slice torn
        into 6 pieces
    6   sprigs parsley, rinsed and patted dry
    1   teaspoon crushed thyme
    1   teaspoon crushed basil
    6   tablespoons melted butter

Insert Steel Blade

Place half of the bread in the Work Bowl; process into crumbs. Place in a large mixing bowl. Process remaining bread.

Wipe the Work Bowl dry with paper toweling. Add parsley to the Work Bowl; mince. Add thyme and basil; process to combine.

Add herb mixture and melted butter to the bread crumbs; mix well.

Lamb Patties

Makes 4 servings.

- 1¼ pounds lamb shoulder, cut into ¾-inch pieces
- 1 teaspoon salt
- ¼ teaspoon white pepper
- ¼ teaspoon crushed oregano
- ¼ teaspoon crushed basil
- 1 medium onion, quartered
- 2 slices dry white bread, each slice torn into 6 pieces
- 2 extra large eggs, lightly beaten
- 3 tablespoons butter
- 2 tablespoons vegetable oil

Insert Steel Blade

Add lamb, salt, pepper, oregano, and basil to the Work Bowl; mince 7 seconds. Place lamb in a large mixing bowl.

Add onion to the Work Bowl; mince 5 seconds. Add to lamb.

Add bread to Work Bowl; process to make crumbs. Add the bread crumbs and the eggs to the lamb; blend thoroughly.

Heat the butter and the oil in a large frying pan. Shape lamb into patties. Fry over medium heat until no longer pink.

Sausage Skillet

Makes 6 to 8 servings.

- 1½ pounds pork sausage, casing removed; cut into 1-inch pieces
- 5 large potatoes, cooked partially, peeled, and quartered
- 1 small head cabbage, cored, and cut into processor-sized wedges
- ½ teaspoon salt
- ½ teaspoon black pepper
- 2 teaspoons caraway seed
- ½ cup dry white wine

Insert Steel Blade

Place half of the sausage in the Work Bowl; process to crumble. Place sausage in a large frying pan. Crumble remaining sausage; place in frying pan.

Brown sausage, stirring often. Drain fat.

Insert Slicing Disc

Fit potatoes into the Feed Tube; slice. Arrange over sausage.

Fit cabbage wedges into the Feed Tube; slice. Arrange cabbage over potatoes.

Sprinkle on salt, pepper, and caraway seed; mix lightly.

Drizzle wine over all. Cover and simmer about 40 minutes until all the ingredients are cooked, stirring occasionally.

Vitello Tonnato

Makes 8 servings.

- 1 large onion, quartered
- 3 large carrots, peeled and cut into 1-inch pieces
- 4 ribs celery, trimmed and cut into 4-inch lengths
- 2½ pounds veal roast
- 1 cup water
- ½ cup white wine
- 3 bay leaves
- ¾ teaspoon salt
- ¼ teaspoon black pepper

Insert Slicing Disc

Fit onion into the Feed Tube; slice with light pressure; set aside. Fit carrots vertically into Feed Tube; slice; set aside. Fit celery vertically into the Feed Tube; slice.

Place onion, carrots, and celery in a Dutch oven. Place veal on top of vegetables. Add remaining ingredients. Bring to a boil. Reduce heat, cover, and simmer for 1½ hours or until veal is tender. Cool. Prepare Sauce.

Sauce

- 1 2-ounce can anchovies
- 1 6½-ounce can tuna, packed in oil, drained; reserve oil
- 2 tablespoons lemon juice
- ¼ cup capers
- 1 medium lemon, ends removed
- 5 sprigs parsley, rinsed and patted dry

Combine reserved tuna oil and enough vegetable oil to measure ¼ cup.

Insert Steel Blade

Place anchovies, tuna, and oils in the Work Bowl; purée. Add lemon juice; blend well. Pour sauce over veal. Garnish with capers.

Insert slicing Disc

Fit lemon into the bottom of the Feed Tube; slice with medium pressure. Arrange lemon around the veal. Wash and dry the Work Bowl.

Insert Steel Blade

Place parsley in the Work Bowl; mince. Sprinkle parsley over veal. Serve chilled.

Breaded Veal

Makes 6 servings.

- 6 veal cutlets
- 4 sprigs parsley, rinsed and patted dry
- 3 cloves garlic
- 3 slices dry white bread, each slice torn into 6 pieces
- 6 ounces Parmesan cheese at room temperature, cut in ½-inch pieces
- ¾ teaspoon salt
- ½ teaspoon black pepper
- ¼ cup unbleached all-purpose flour
- 3 eggs. lightly beaten
- ¼ cup milk
- 5 tablespoons vegetable oil
- 3 tablespoons butter
- 2 medium lemons, ends trimmed

Pound veal with a mallet to flatten. Set aside.

Insert Steel Blade

Place parsley in the Work Bowl; mince; set aside. With the processor running, drop the garlic through the Feed Tube; mince; set aside. Add bread to Work Bowl; process to make crumbs. Place in a shallow bowl or on a plate.

With the procesor running, drop the cheese through the Feed Tube; process until fine. Add garlic, cheese, salt, and pepper to the crumbs; mix well.

Place flour on a sheet of waxed paper. Combine eggs and milk in a shallow dish. Heat oil and butter in a large frying pan. Dip each cutlet in flour; then dip into the egg mixture; then dip into the bread crumb mixture. Fry on both sides until no longer pink.

Insert Slicing Disc

Fit lemon into the bottom of the Feed Tube. Attach cover to the Work Bowl; slice with medium pressure. Garnish veal with lemon slices.

Sausage Bake

Makes 4 servings.

- 4 medium potatoes, peeled, quartered lengthwise, and partially cooked
- 2 large onions, quartered
- 4 large red Delicious apples, peeled, cored, and quartered
- 6 tablespoons butter
- 1½ pounds Polish sausage, casings removed and cut into 1-inch pieces

Insert Slicing Disc

Stand potatoes in the Feed Tube; slice; set aside. Fit the onions into the Feed Tube; slice with light pressure; set aside. Lay the apples in the Feed tube; slice; set aside.

Heat 2 tablespoons of the butter in a large frying pan. Fry the sausage until browned; drain fat. Remove sausage from the frying pan; set aside. Heat remaining butter in the same frying pan. Sauté potatoes and onions until potatoes are almost tender, about 5 minutes, stirring occasionally. Add apples and cook for 3 minutes. Return sausage to frying pan; mix well.

Osso Buco

Braised Veal Shanks

Makes 8 servings.

- 3 cloves garlic
- 1 large onion, cut into 6 pieces
- 6 sprigs parsley, rinsed and patted dry
  Rind from half a small lemon
- 1 cup unbleached all-purpose flour
- 1 pound mushrooms, trimmed
- 3 carrots, peeled and trimmed to even lengths
- 1 teaspoon salt
- 7 pounds veal shanks including marrow, cut into 1½-inch pieces (Ask your butcher to help.)
- 5 tablespoons butter
- 2 tablespoons vegetable oil
- 2 cups dry red wine
- 1 cup chicken bouillon

Insert Steel Blade

With the processor running, drop the garlic through the Feed Tube; mince. Drop the onion through the Feed Tube; mince; set aside.

Add parsley to Work Bowl; mince; set aside.

Add lemon rind and flour to Work Bowl; mince rind. Place on a sheet of waxed paper.

Insert Slicing Disc

Place mushrooms randomly in the Feed Tube; slice; set aside. Stand carrots vertically in the Feed Tube; slice; set aside.

Sprinkle salt over veal shanks. Roll shanks in the lemon-flour mixture.

Heat the butter and oil in a large saucepan. Add the garlic, onion, mushrooms, and carrots; sauté for 2 minutes. Remove from pan; set aside. Brown veal shanks on all sides. Return vegetables to frying pan. Add wine, bouillon, and parsley. Cover and simmer for 1½ hours or until tender. Serve with noodles.

Couscous

Makes 8 to 10 servings.

- 2 cloves garlic
- 1 large onion, cut into 6 pieces
- ¼ cup olive oil
- 3 tablespoons butter
- 2 3½-pound chickens, cut into serving pieces
- 1 16-ounce can tomatoes, including juice
- ½ teaspoon coriander
- 1 teaspoon ground cumin
- ½ teaspoon salt
- ½ teaspoon black pepper
- 3 large carrots, trimmed and cut into 1-inch chunks
- 1 cup stuffed green olives
- 4 large turnips, peeled and quartered
- 4 large potatoes, peeled and quartered
- 1 1-pound box pitted prunes

Insert Steel Blade

With the processor running, drop the garlic through the Feed Tube; mince 5 seconds. Add onion; mince 5 to 7 seconds; set aside.

Heat olive oil and butter in a Dutch oven. Add garlic and onion; sauté for 2 minutes. Add chicken; brown on all sides. Remove chicken and set aside. Reserve pan drippings.

Insert Steel Blade

Add tomatoes to Work Bowl; chop roughly.

Add tomatoes, coriander, cumin, salt, and pepper to pan drippings.

Insert Grating Disc

Fit carrots into the Feed Tube; grate. Add carrots to pan.

Insert Slicing Disc

Place olives randomly in the Feed Tube; slice with light pressure. Add olives to pan.

Place turnips in the Feed Tube; slice with medium pressure. Add turnips to pan.

Place potatoes in the Feed Tube; slice with medium pressure. Add potatoes, along with prunes, to the pan.

Add reserved tomato juice and enough water to cover vegetables.

Simmer for 25 minutes. Return chicken to pan; mix lightly. Simmer until vegetables and chicken are tender, about 20 minutes.

Prepare Couscous

- 1 1-pound box precooked couscous (Available at specialty food stores.)
  Boiling water or liquid from above stew
- 1 teaspoon salt

Measure amount of couscous in the box. Place in a large mixing bowl. Add an equal amount of boiling water or stewing liquid along with the salt; toss lightly. Let stand for 5 minutes.

Mound couscous in the center of a deep serving bowl or platter. Arrange chicken and vegetables around the edge of the couscous.

Chicken Cacciatore

Makes 4 servings.

- 4 sprigs parsley, rinsed and patted dry
- 2 cloves garlic
- 1 16-ounce can tomatoes; quarter tomatoes, reserve juice
- 1 large onion, cut into 6 pieces
- 1 cup unbleached all-purpose flour
- 1 teaspoon salt
- ½ teaspoon black pepper
- 1½ pounds chicken, cut into serving pieces
- ½ cup olive oil
- 1 teaspoon salt
- 1½ teaspoons crushed oregano
- ½ teaspoon black pepper
  Pasta (Recipe on page 54)

Insert Steel Blade

Place parsley in the Work Bowl; mince 10 seconds; set aside. With the machine running, drop the garlic down the Feed Tube; mince about 5 seconds; set aside. Add tomatoes and reserved juice; chop roughly; set aside.

Insert Slicing Disc

Fit onion in the Feed Tube; slice with light pressure; set aside.

Sprinkle flour on a sheet of waxed paper. Mix in the salt and pepper. Coat the chicken with seasoned flour. Heat oil in a large frying pan or Dutch oven. Add garlic and onion; sauté for 1 minute. Add chicken and brown on all sides. Combine parsley, tomatoes, salt, oregano, and pepper. Add tomato mixture to the chicken. Simmer, uncovered, for 25 minutes. If liquid becomes too thick, stir in additional water, ½ cup at a time. Serve over hot pasta.

Chicken Quenelles with Herbed Tomato Sauce or Light Wine Sauce

Makes 4 servings.

  2 egg whites
  1 pound chicken breasts, boned, skinned and
    cut into ¾-inch pieces
  1 teaspoon salt
  ½ teaspoon white pepper
  ¼ teaspoon ground nutmeg
  1¾ cups heavy cream

Generously butter a large frying pan.

Insert Steel Blade

Drop egg whites into the Work Bowl; process for 8 seconds.

Place chicken in the Work Bowl; process until puréed. Add salt, pepper, and nutmeg; process just to combine.

With the processor running, pour half of the cream through the Feed Tube in a steady stream. Stop motor. Check to see if the mixture will hold its shape. If not, blend in remaining cream, 3 tablespoons at a time. Continue testing to see if the mixture will hold its shape. It may not be necessary to use all of the cream.

Dip 2 tablespoons into cold water. Barely fill one of the spoons with chicken mixture. Place the other spoon over the top. Gently mold chicken mixture between the spoons. Carefully slide quenelles onto the buttered frying pan. Fill pan with a single layer, allowing room for expansion. Slowly pour enough salted water in from the side of the pan to cover quenelles halfway. Simmer, turning once, until quenelles are firm, about 8 to 10 minutes. Remove with slotted spoon; drain on paper toweling. Cover quenelles with aluminum foil.

Prepare Sauce. Drizzle over quenelles.

Herbed Tomato Sauce

  1 teaspoon crushed tarragon
  1 teaspoon chives, cut into 1-inch pieces
  2 tablespoons lemon juice
  2 eggs
  ¼ teaspoon salt
  ¼ cup tomato sauce
  6 tablespoons melted butter
  6 tablespoons peanut oil

Insert Steel Blade

Place tarragon, chives, lemon juice, eggs, salt, and tomato sauce in the Work Bowl; pulse 5 times with On-Off control or use pulse technique; run processor nonstop for 10 seconds. With the machine running, pour butter and oil through the Feed Tube; combine for 15 seconds. Heat sauce in a saucepan.

Light Wine Sauce

  1 small onion, quartered
  ½ teaspoon crushed tarragon
  ½ cup heavy cream
  ¼ cup butter, melted
  2 tablespoons white wine

Insert Steel Blade

Drop onion through the Feed Tube; mince about 5 to 7 seconds. Add tarragon and cream; pulse 4 times with the On-Off control or use the pulse technique. With the processor running, pour the butter and wine through the Feed Tube; process to combine. Heat sauce in a saucepan.

Mexican Chicken with Molé Sauce

Makes 4 to 6 servings.

  ¼ cup vegetable oil
  3 tablespoons butter
  1 3½-pound chicken, cut into serving pieces
  ½ medium green pepper, seeded and
    cut into 1-inch chunks
  2 cloves garlic
  1 medium onion, quartered
  1 16-ounce can tomatoes, quartered,
    reserve juice
  6 tablespoons blanched, slivered almonds
  2 tablespoons cocoa
  1 teaspoon salt
  2 teaspoons sesame seed
  1 teaspoon chili powder
  ½ teaspoon ground cinnamon
  3 tablespoons vegetable oil

Heat the ¼ cup oil and butter in a 4-quart saucepan. Brown chicken on all sides. Fry until tender. Drain on paper toweling. Set aside.

Insert Steel Blade

With the processor running, drop the green pepper through the Feed Tube; chop; set aside. Wipe out the Work Bowl with a damp towel.

With the processor running, drop garlic through the Feed Tube; mince 5 seconds. Scrape sides of the Work Bowl with a rubber spatula. Add onion; mince 5 to 7 seconds; set aside.

Add tomatoes and liquid to Work Bowl; chop; set aside.

Wash and dry the Work Bowl. Add almonds; grind 10 seconds. Add cocoa, salt, sesame seed, chili powder, and cinnamon; process just to combine. Return tomatoes to Work Bowl; combine for 10 seconds.

Heat the 3 tablespoons oil in a small saucepan. Add garlic and onion; sauté for 3 minutes. Add pepper; sauté for 2 minutes. Add tomato mixture; simmer for 5 minutes, stirring occasionally.

When ready to serve, reheat chicken and place on a serving platter. Pour heated molé sauce over chicken.

Chicken with Pineapple
Makes 4 servings.

- 2 cloves garlic
- ¾ cup macadamia nuts or dry roasted peanuts
- ½ small pineapple, trimmed, cored and quartered
- 1 medium onion, quartered
- 3 ribs celery, trimmed and cut into 4-inch lengths
- 2 whole chicken breasts, boned, chilled until partially frozen, and cut into Feed Tube-size pieces
- ¼ cup vegetable oil
- ¼ cup soy sauce
- 1 teaspoon brown sugar
- ½ cup chicken bouillon
- 2 tablespoons cornstarch
  Rice

Insert Steel Blade

With the machine running, drop the garlic through the Feed Tube; mince 5 seconds; set aside. Add nuts; chop roughly 10 seconds; set aside.

Insert Slicing Disc

Fit pineapple into the Feed Tube; slice with medium pressure. Process all pineapple; set aside.

Slice onion with light pressure; set aside.

Fit celery vertically into the Feed Tube; slice with light pressure; set aside.

Fit chicken pieces into the Feed Tube; slice with firm pressure; set aside.

Heat oil in a wok or a heavy frying pan. Stir-fry garlic, onion, and celery until tender-crisp, about 30 seconds. Add chicken; stir-fry until chicken is cooked. Stir in soy sauce, brown sugar, and ¼ cup of the bouillon.

Combine remaining ¼ cup of the bouillon with the cornstarch; stir into chicken mixture. Stir until the mixture begins to thicken. Add pineapple; stir-fry 2 minutes. Serve over hot rice. Garnish with chopped nuts.

Chinese Chicken with Green Peppers
Makes 6 servings.

- ½ teaspoon minced, hot red chilies
- 2 tablespoons soy sauce
- 1 tablespoon sherry
- 1 teaspoon granulated sugar
- 2 cloves garlic
- 1 ¼-inch slice fresh gingerroot, skin removed
- 3 green onions, cut into 1-inch pieces
- 3 whole chicken breasts, boned and partially frozen
- 1 egg white, lightly beaten
- 1 teaspoon cornstarch
- ¼ teaspoon salt
- ¼ teaspoon white pepper
- 2 large green peppers, halved and seeded
- ½ cup sliced bamboo shoots
- 6 tablespoons peanut oil
- ½ cup unsalted roasted peanuts

Combine chilies, soy sauce, sherry, and sugar in a small bowl; set aside.

Insert Steel Blade

With the processor running, drop the garlic and gingerroot through the Feed Tube; mince 5 seconds. Add green onions; mince 6 seconds; set aside.

Insert Slicing Disc

Fit chicken vertically into the Feed Tube; slice with heavy pressure; set aside. Combine egg white, cornstarch, salt, and pepper; sprinkle mixture over chicken. Let stand 10 minutes.

Curl peppers into the bottom of the Feed Tube; slice with light pressure; set aside. (If using whole bamboo shoots, insert in Feed Tube; slice with light pressure.)

Heat oil in a wok or a large frying pan. Add peanuts and stir-fry for 1 minute. Remove peanuts with a slotted spoon; drain on paper toweling. Add garlic and gingerroot; stir-fry for 30 seconds. Add chicken; stir-fry until chicken is white. Stir in green onions, green peppers, bamboo shoots, and peanuts. Stir in soy sauce mixture. Heat through. Serve over rice.

Cape Cod Oyster Pie

Makes 6 to 8 servings.

Crust

1¼ cups unbleached all-purpose flour
¼ teaspoon salt
4 tablespoons butter, cut into ½-inch pieces
   and brought to room temperature
2 tablespoons vegetable shortening
5 to 7 tablespoons ice water

Insert Steel Blade

Place flour, salt, butter, and shortening in the Work Bowl. Process until mixture is the consistency of cornmeal. With the machine running, pour water through the Feed Tube. Dough will form a ball around the center post. Stop machine after the water is absorbed, even if the dough has not formed a ball. Turn dough out of Work Bowl. Gather it into a ball. Cover with plastic wrap. Refrigerate for 30 minutes.

Sauce

4 tablespoons butter
4 tablespoons unbleached all-purpose flour
1½ cups milk or light cream

Heat butter in a small saucepan. Whisk in flour. Whisk in milk or cream. Cook until sauce thickens, stirring constantly. Remove from heat. Set aside.

Filling

3 sprigs parsley, rinsed and patted dry
3 medium-large potatoes, peeled, boiled, cooled,
   and cut in half vertically
1 medium onion, quartered
4 ribs celery, trimmed and cut into 4-inch lengths

Insert Steel Blade

Place parsley in Work Bowl; mince 10 to 12 seconds. Remove from Work Bowl and set aside.

Insert Slicing Disc

Fit potatoes into the Feed Tube; slice and set aside. Fit onion into the Feed Tube; slice with light pressure and set aside. Arrange celery vertically in the Feed Tube; slice.

To Assemble

3 cups small oysters
½ teaspoon salt
¼ teaspoon white pepper

Butter a 10-inch deep-dish pie plate. Layer half of the potatoes, half of the onions, half the oysters, and half the celery. Sprinkle on salt and pepper. Repeat layers with remaining ingredients. Pour sauce over all. Roll out crust on a lightly floured board. Cover pie with crust. Crimp edges. Make decorative design in the top. Preheat oven to 350°. Bake for 40 minutes or until crust is golden. Cool for 5 minutes.

Trout with Spinach-Mushroom Stuffing

Makes 4 servings.

2 cloves garlic
1 small onion, cut in half
2 slices dry bread, each slice torn into 6 pieces
½ 10-ounce package frozen spinach,
   thawed, blanched, and drained
1 cup small mushrooms, trimmed
3 tablespoons butter
½ teaspoon salt
½ teaspoon white pepper
½ teaspoon crushed tarragon
¼ teaspoon crushed thyme
1 3½-pound trout, cleaned, leaving
   head and tail intact
2 tablespoons butter, cut into 4 pieces

Insert Steel Blade

With the processor running, drop the garlic and onion through the Feed Tube; process until minced, 5 to 6 seconds; set aside. Add bread to Work Bowl; process into crumbs, about 10 to 15 seconds.

Add spinach to Work Bowl; mince and set aside. Add mushrooms; chop and set aside.

Heat butter in a large frying pan. Add garlic, onion, and mushrooms; sauté for 2 minutes, stirring occasionally. Add spinach; sauté 1 minute. Stir in crumbs and seasonings; simmer 2 minutes.

Butter a baking sheet. Preheat oven to 350°. Place trout on a baking sheet or large casserole. Spoon stuffing into cavity. Place remaining stuffing around fish. Dot top of fish with butter. Bake uncovered for 40 minutes or until the fish flakes easily. Let stand 5 minutes before serving.

White Clam Sauce

Makes 6 servings.

- 1 large onion, quartered
- 2 cloves garlic
- 3 sprigs parsley, rinsed and patted dry
- ½ pound Romano cheese, room temperature, cut into ½-inch pieces
- ¼ cup vegetable oil
- 3 tablespoons unbleached all-purpose flour
- ½ teaspoon crushed basil
- ½ teaspoon crushed oregano
- ⅛ teaspoon ground nutmeg
- 2 6½-ounce cans minced clams, drained; reserve liquid
- ½ cup milk

Insert Slicing Disc

Place onion in Feed Tube; slice with light pressure. Set aside.

Insert Steel Blade

With the processor running, drop the garlic through the Feed Tube; mince 5 seconds. Add parsley; mince 10 seconds. Set aside. With the machine running, drop the cheese through the Feed Tube; process until finely minced. Set aside.

Heat oil in a 2-quart saucepan. Add onion, garlic, and parsley; sauté for 1 minute. Add clam juice and flour. Bring to a boil; reduce to a simmer. Add cheese, seasonings, clams, and milk to the vegetables; combine. Simmer for 2 minutes or until thick. Serve over linguine.

Shrimp with Remoulade Sauce

Makes 8 servings.

- 2 cloves garlic
- 4 sprigs parsley, rinsed and patted dry
- 4 ribs celery, trimmed and cut into 4-inch lengths
- 2 12-ounce cans beer
- 3 tablespoons lemon juice
- 2 bay leaves
- ½ teaspoon salt
- ¼ teaspoon black pepper
- 2½ pounds shrimp, rinsed and drained
- 1 small head iceberg lettuce

Insert Steel Blade

With the processor running, drop the garlic through the Feed Tube; process until minced, about 5 seconds. Remove from Work Bowl and set aside. Add parsley to the Work Bowl; process until minced, 10 to 12 seconds; set aside.

Insert Slicing Disc

Fit celery vertically into the Feed Tube; slice with light pressure; set aside.

Place garlic, parsley, celery, beer, lemon juice, bay leaves, salt, and pepper in a 3-quart saucepan; bring to a boil. Reduce heat to a simmer. Add shrimp; simmer for 3 minutes or until shrimp are opaque. Drain shrimp; shell and devein, leaving tails intact. Chill thoroughly.

When ready to serve, cut lettuce into Feed Tube-size pieces.

Fit lettuce wedges into the Feed Tube; slice with light pressure. Arrange lettuce on 8 serving plates. Arrange shrimp over lettuce. Drizzle Remoulade Sauce over shrimp.

Remoulade Sauce

- 4 sprigs parsley, rinsed and patted dry
- 2 green onions, cut into 1½-inch pieces; include tops
- 2 tablespoons capers
- 1 teaspoon wine vinegar
- 1 cup Mayonnaise (Recipe on page 27)
- ½ teaspoon chervil
- ½ teaspoon tarragon
- ½ teaspoon salt
- ⅛ teaspoon white pepper

Insert Steel Blade

Place parsley in Work Bowl; process until minced, 10 to 12 seconds. Add green onions; process until minced, 5 to 7 seconds. Add capers, wine vinegar, and Mayonnaise; process until all the ingredients are blended, about 4 seconds. Add remaining ingredients; process until combined, about 4 seconds. Remove sauce to a bowl. Cover and chill until ready to serve.

Shrimp Creole

Makes 6 to 8 servings.

- 3 cloves garlic
- 1 large onion, quartered
- 1 16-ounce can tomatoes, cut in half, include juice
- 2 large bell peppers, cut in half and seeded
- 3 tablespoons vegetable oil
- 3 tablespoons butter
- ¼ cup chili sauce
- ½ teaspoon salt
- 1 teaspoon honey
- 3 bay leaves
- 1 pound large shrimp, peeled and deveined; leave tail intact

Insert Steel Blade

With the processor running, drop the garlic through the Feed Tube; process until minced. Add onion to the Work Bowl; mince about 5 seconds. Remove from Work Bowl and set aside. Add tomatoes; chop roughly; set aside.

Insert Slicing Disc

Curl peppers into the bottom of the Feed Tube; slice and set aside.

Heat oil and butter in a large frying pan. Sauté garlic, onion, and peppers for 3 minutes, stirring occasionally. Add tomatoes, juice, chili sauce, salt, honey, and bay leaves; stir to combine. Simmer, uncovered, for 3 to 5 minutes. Add shrimp; simmer until the shrimp are done. Discard bay leaves. Serve over hot rice.

Fish Fingers

Makes 4 servings.

    1 large onion, quartered
    8 tablespoons butter, divided
    2 cups cooked fish, boned and flaked
    1 cup mashed potatoes
    1 teaspoon salt
    ½ teaspoon white pepper
    ¼ teaspoon dillweed
    2 extra large eggs
    ¼ cup heavy cream
    4 tablespoons vegetable oil

Insert Slicing Disc

Fit onion in the Feed Tube; slice with light pressure.

Heat 4 tablespoons of the butter in a small frying pan. Add onion; sauté for 2 minutes. Set aside.

Insert Steel Blade

Add half of the onion mixture, 1 cup fish, ½ cup potatoes, ½ teaspoon salt, ¼ teaspoon pepper, ⅛ teaspoon dillweed, 1 egg, 2 tablespoons heavy cream; purée. Place fish mixture in a mixing bowl. Purée remaining ingredients. Combine all ingredients in the mixing bowl.

Heat remaining butter and oil in a large frying pan. Shape fish mixture into 1 x 3-inch fingers. Fry until golden brown, turning once. Drain on paper toweling.

Scallops with White Wine Sauce

Makes 6 servings.

    3 shallots, cut in half
    4 sprigs parsley, rinsed and patted dry
    1 carrot, pared and cut into 1-inch lengths
    3 tablespoons butter
    1 pound small bay scallops
    2 tablespoons all-purpose flour
    ½ cup dry white wine
    ½ cup heavy cream

Insert Steel Blade

With the processor running, drop the shallots through the Feed Tube; mince. Remove from Work Bowl and set aside. Wipe Work Bowl dry. Add parsley; mince 10 to 15 seconds. Remove from Work Bowl and set aside.

Insert Grating Disc

Arrange carrot in the Feed Tube; grate and set aside.

Heat butter in a large frying pan. Sauté shallots and carrot for 1 minute. Add scallops; sauté until opaque. Remove scallops with a slotted spoon. Whisk in flour until liquid is absorbed. Stir in wine and cream; whisk until thickened. Add parsley.

Return scallops to pan. Heat through. Serve over a bed of green buttered noodles.

Salmon Patties

Makes 3 to 4 servings.

    1 medium onion, quartered
    1 slice dry white bread; tear into 6 pieces
    1 15-ounce can salmon; drain, remove any bones, break into large chunks
    1 extra large egg
    ½ teaspoon salt
    ¼ teaspoon white pepper
    3 tablespoons butter
    2 teaspoons vegetable oil

Insert Steel Blade

Place onion in Work Bowl; mince 5 seconds. Add bread; process to make crumbs. Add salmon, egg, salt, and pepper. Process 8 seconds until combined.

Heat butter and oil in a 12-inch frying pan. Form salmon mixture into 3-inch patties. Fry on both sides until golden brown. Drain on paper toweling.

Breads and Pasta

Christmas Fruit Bread

Makes 10 to 12 servings.

- ¼ cup candied orange peel
- ¼ cup golden raisins
- ¼ cup candied cherries
- 1 cup flour
- ¼ cup warm water (105 to 115° F.)
- 1 package active dry yeast
- 1 teaspoon granulated sugar
- 2 cups unbleached all-purpose flour
- ¼ cup granulated sugar
- ½ teaspoon salt
- ½ cup milk, scalded and cooled
- 1 teaspoon vanilla
- 2 egg yolks, at room temperature
- 4 tablespoons melted butter, cooled to room temperature
- 1 egg, lightly beaten
- 1 tablespoon water
  Confectioners' sugar

Insert Steel Blade

Place orange peel, raisins, cherries and the 1 cup flour in the Work Bowl. Chop 3 seconds. Remove from Work Bowl and set aside.

Wash Work Bowl and blade with hot water; return to the base. Add warm water, yeast, and sugar to the Work Bowl. Pulse 1 minute. Remove cover. Let stand for 5 minutes to proof yeast. Add the 2 cups flour, sugar, and salt; process 3 On-Off pulses. Combine milk, vanilla, egg yolks, and butter. With the processor running, pour milk mixture through the Feed Tube; process to combine, about 6 seconds. A soft dough will form.

Turn dough out of Work Bowl onto a lightly floured surface. Knead until dough is smooth. Place in a greased bowl, turn once to grease top. Cover and let rise for 2 hours in a draft-free area.

Roll out dough into a 10 x 12-inch rectangle. Sprinkle fruit evenly over dough. Roll up from the short side, jelly-roll style. Place on a greased baking sheet. Combine egg and water. Brush over fruit bread. Cover and let rise in a draft-free area for 1 hour. Preheat oven to 375°. Bake for 45 minutes or until bread tests done. Sprinkle with confectioners' sugar. Cool.

Pecan Rolls

Makes 1 dozen.

- 1 cup whole pecans
- ½ cup milk
- 4 tablespoons butter
- ⅓ cup granulated sugar
- ½ teaspoon salt
- 1 large egg at room temperature, lightly beaten
- ¼ cup warm water (105 to 115° F.)
- 1 package active dry yeast
- 1 teaspoon granulated sugar
- 2½ to 3 cups unbleached all-purpose flour
- 3 tablespoons melted butter
- 1 teaspoon ground cinnamon
- 6 tablespoons granulated sugar
- ½ cup packed dark brown sugar

Insert Steel Blade

Place pecans in Work Bowl; chop roughly. (Processor will be noisy.) Set pecans aside.

Pour milk into a saucepan; scald. Add the 4 tablespoons butter, sugar, and salt; stir until butter melts. Cool to room temperature. Stir in egg; set aside. Pour water into a measuring cup. Sprinkle yeast and sugar over water; stir to dissolve yeast. Place in a draft-free area about 5 minutes.

Add milk and yeast mixtures to the Work Bowl. Pulse 1 time. Add 1 cup of the flour; pulse 2 times. Add remaining flour; process 20 seconds. Dough should gather around the center post. Turn dough out of Work Bowl onto a lightly floured board; gather into a ball.

Place dough in a greased bowl; turn to grease top. Cover with a damp towel. Place in a draft-free area until double in bulk, about 1½ hours. Turn out onto a lightly floured surface. Roll out into an 8 x 16-inch rectangle. Brush the top with melted butter. Combine cinnamon and sugar. Sprinkle over dough. Roll up jelly-roll fashion from the long side. Cut into 12 pieces. Generously grease a 12-cup muffin pan. Sprinkle brown sugar in the bottom of each pan. Divide pecans among pans. Place a piece of dough, cut-side down, in each pan. Cover and let rise for 30 minutes in a draft-free area. Preheat oven to 375°. Bake for 15 minutes. Invert rolls on a baking rack to cool.

Oatmeal Bread

Makes 1 loaf.

    1   cup boiling water
    1   cup quick-cooking oatmeal
    1   package active dry yeast
    1   teaspoon granulated sugar
    ¼   cup warm water (105 to 115° F.)
    ½   teaspoon salt
    2   tablespoons vegetable oil
    2   tablespoons honey
    2½ cups unbleached all-purpose flour or bread flour

Combine water and oatmeal; blend thoroughly. Cool to room temperature. Pour yeast and sugar into warm water; stir to dissolve yeast. Place in a draft-free area to proof, about 5 minutes.

Insert Steel Blade

Place oatmeal and yeast mixtures in Work Bowl. Pulse 3 times. Add salt, oil, and honey; pulse 3 times. Add 1 cup of the flour; pulse 4 times. Gradually add remaining flour. Pulse until dough gathers around the center post.

Turn dough out onto a lightly floured board; gather dough into a ball. Place dough in a greased bowl; turn dough to grease top. Cover with a damp towel or oiled aluminum foil. Place in a draft-free area until doubled in bulk, about 1½ hours. Shape dough into a loaf. Place in a greased 9 x 5-inch loaf pan. Cover and let rise for 45 minutes in draft-free area. Preheat oven to 350°. Bake for 45 minutes or until bread tests done.

Herb-Filled Bread

Makes 1 loaf.

    ¼   cup loosely packed parsley
    ¼   cup loosely packed basil
    ¼   cup loosely packed tarragon
    ½   cup milk
    ½   teaspoon salt
    3   tablespoons butter, cut into ½-inch pieces
    ½   cup warm water (105 to 115° F.)
    1   package active dry yeast
    1   tablespoon granulated sugar
    3   cups unbleached all-purpose flour

Wash all herbs and dry with paper toweling.

Insert Steel Blade

Place parsley in Work Bowl; mince 10 seconds. Leave parsley in Work Bowl. Add basil and tarragon; mince. Set aside.

Scald milk in a small saucepan. Add salt and butter; stir until butter melts. Cool to room temperature. Pour water into a measuring cup. Sprinkle yeast and sugar over water; stir to dissolve yeast. Place in a draft-free area to proof, about 5 minutes.

Insert Steel Blade

Place milk and yeast mixtures into Work Bowl; pulse 1 time. Add 1 cup of the flour; pulse 2 times. Add remaining flour; process 20 seconds. Dough will gather around the center post. Turn dough out onto a lightly floured board. Gather dough into a ball.

Place dough in a greased bowl; turn dough to grease top. Cover with a damp towel or oiled aluminum foil. Place in a draft-free area until doubled in bulk, about 1¾ hours. Turn out onto a lightly floured board. Roll out into an 8 x 12-inch rectangle. Sprinkle herbs evenly over bread; roll up jelly-roll style from the long side. Fit into a greased 9 x 5-inch loaf pan. Cover with oiled aluminum foil. Let rise for 45 minutes. Preheat oven to 375°. Bake for 35 to 45 minutes or until bread tests done. Cool on a wire rack.

Wheat Germ Bread

Makes 1 loaf.

    ½   cup milk
    ½   cup water
    2   tablespoons butter, cut into ½-inch pieces
    ½   teaspoon salt
    1   tablespoon honey
    1   egg at room temperature, lightly beaten
    ¼   cup warm water (105 to 115° F.)
    1   package active dry yeast
    1   teaspoon honey
    3   cups unbleached all-purpose flour
        or bread flour
    ½   cup wheat germ

Pour milk and water into a small saucepan; scald. Add butter, salt, and honey; stir until the butter melts. Cool to room temperature. Stir in egg.

Insert Steel Blade

Place water, yeast, and honey in the Work Bowl. Pulse 1 time. Remove processor lid. Let the yeast proof, about 5 minutes. Add milk mixture; pulse 1 time. Add 1 cup of the flour; pulse 2 times. Gradually add remaining flour and wheat germ; process for 12 seconds. Dough will gather around the center post. Turn dough out onto a lightly floured board; knead for 30 seconds. Gather into a ball.

Place dough in a greased bowl; turn dough to grease top of dough. Cover with a damp towel. Let rise in a draft-free area until doubled in bulk, about 1½ hours. Punch down dough. Place on a lightly floured board; knead for 1 minute. Form into a loaf. Butter a 9 x 5 x 3-inch loaf pan. Place dough in the pan. Cover and let rise in a draft-free area for 45 minutes. Preheat oven to 375°. Bake for 40 minutes or until bread tests done. Cool on a wire rack.

Boston Brown Bread

Makes 1 loaf.

  1 egg
  3 tablespoons granulated sugar
  1 cup light or dark molasses
  ¾ cup buttermilk
  ½ teaspoon salt
  1 cup whole wheat flour
  1 cup unbleached all-purpose flour
  ½ teaspoon baking soda
  ½ teaspoon baking powder
  ½ cup dark raisins

Grease a clean 2-pound coffee can or use two 1-pound cans.

Insert Steel Blade

Place egg, sugar, molasses, and buttermilk in the Work Bowl; process 6 seconds. Add salt, flours, baking soda, and baking powder; process 4 seconds. Add raisins; pulse one time to blend.

Pour mixture into prepared pan, scraping sides of the Work Bowl with a spatula. Bake at 350° 45 to 55 minutes or until bread tests done.

Breadsticks

Makes about 2 dozen.

  ¾ cup warm water (105 to 115° F.)
  1 package active dry yeast
  1 teaspoon granulated sugar
  2¼ cups unbleached all-purpose flour
  3 tablespoons vegetable oil
  ½ teaspoon salt
  1 egg
  1 egg, lightly beaten
  ¼ cup sesame seed

Pour water into a measuring cup. Sprinkle yeast and sugar over water; stir to dissolve yeast. Place in a draft-free area to proof, about 5 minutes.

Insert Steel Blade

Add flour, oil, and salt to Work Bowl; pulse to combine. Add yeast mixture and the whole egg; process until dough gathers around center post, about 10 seconds.

Place dough on a lightly floured surface. Gather it into a ball. Place dough in a greased bowl; turn to grease top of dough. Cover with a damp towel or oiled aluminum foil. Let rise until doubled in bulk, about 1½ hours. Punch down dough. Divide dough into 25 pieces. Grease a baking sheet. Roll each ball into the shape of a pencil. Place on baking sheet. Brush each breadstick with beaten egg; sprinkle on sesame seed. Cover loosely with a towel. Let rise for 30 minutes. Preheat oven to 325°. Bake 25 to 30 minutes or until breadsticks are golden brown.

Applesauce Bread with Raisins

Makes 8 servings.

  6 tablespoons butter, cut into ½-inch pieces
  ½ cup packed brown sugar
  ¼ cup granulated sugar
  1 egg
  1 teaspoon vanilla
  ¾ cup applesauce
  1 teaspoon ground cinnamon
  ½ teaspoon ground nutmeg
  ¼ teaspoon ground cloves
  2 cups unbleached all-purpose flour
  2 teaspoons baking soda
  1 teaspoon baking powder
  1 cup golden raisins

Preheat oven to 350°. Grease a 9 x 5 x 3-inch loaf pan.

Insert Steel Blade

Place butter and both sugars in the Work Bowl. Process about 10 seconds until light and fluffy. Add egg, vanilla, and applesauce; process for 4 seconds. Add remaining ingredients, except raisins; process for 4 seconds. Add raisins; process 1 second.

Pour batter into prepared pan. Bake for 45 minutes or until bread tests done. Cool on a wire rack. Slice and serve with sweetened cream cheese.

Irish Soda Bread

Makes 1 loaf.

- ¾ cup granulated sugar
- Rind of ½ lemon
- 2 eggs
- 3 tablespoons melted butter
- 1¾ cups buttermilk
- 2¼ cups unbleached all-purpose flour or bread flour
- 1½ teaspoons baking soda
- 1½ teaspoons baking powder
- ½ teaspoon salt
- 1 cup dark raisins

Insert Steel Blade

Place ½ cup of the sugar and the lemon rind in the Work Bowl; process until the rind is finely minced, about 6 seconds. Add remaining sugar and eggs; process for 10 seconds. Add butter and buttermilk; process for 15 seconds. Add flour, baking soda, baking powder, and salt; process for 5 seconds. Add raisins; process for 1 second.

Grease a 9 x 5 x 3-inch loaf pan. Preheat oven to 350°. Bake for 50 minutes or until the bread tests done. Remove from the pan; cool.

Brioche

Makes 1 brioche.

- ½ cup warm water (105 to 115° F.)
- 1 package active dry yeast
- 1 teaspoon granulated sugar
- ½ cup butter, cut into ½-inch pieces and brought to room temperature
- 3 tablespoons granulated sugar
- ½ teaspoon salt
- 3 eggs
- 2¼ cups unbleached all-purpose flour or bread flour
- 1 tablespoon water

Pour water into a measuring cup. Sprinkle yeast and the 1 teaspoon sugar over water; stir to dissolve yeast. Let stand in a draft-free area to proof, about 5 minutes.

Insert Steel Blade

Place butter, 3 tablespoons sugar, and salt in the Work Bowl. Process nonstop for 30 seconds. Add yeast mixture; process for 6 seconds. Add 2 of the eggs; process for 6 seconds. Add 1¼ cups of the flour; process only until it is just mixed. Add remaining flour. Do *not* overprocess. Turn dough into a greased bowl; turn to grease top of dough. Cover with a damp towel or greased aluminum foil. Let stand in a

draft-free area for 1½ hours, until doubled in bulk. Punch down dough. Butter a 6-cup brioche pan (available at gourmet food stores) or individual brioche pans. Tear off a walnut-size piece of dough and form into a small ball; set aside. Smooth remaining dough into a ball. Place in the prepared pan. Use your thumb to press a slight indentation in the top of the dough. Press small ball of dough lightly into the top of the large dough.

Insert Plastic Blade

Add the remaining egg and the water to Work Bowl; pulse 5 times. Brush top of the dough with egg wash.

Cover dough with oiled aluminum foil. Let rise for 2 hours in a draft-free area. Preheat oven to 375°. Bake for 45 minutes or until golden brown and bread tests done. Cool.

Egg Pasta

Makes enough pasta for 6 servings.

- 1¾ cups unbleached all-purpose flour
- ¾ cup instant flour
- ½ teaspoon salt
- 3 extra large eggs
- 2 tablespoons olive oil

Insert Steel Blade

Place flours, salt, eggs, and olive oil in the Work Bowl; process about 12 seconds to combine. Remove dough from the Work Bowl. Dust with flour. Wrap in plastic wrap. Let stand at room temperature for 20 minutes. Knead the dough on a lightly floured board for 30 seconds. Divide dough into 4 equal parts.

Roll out each part into an 8 x 10-inch rectangle on a lightly floured board. Roll up dough from the long end, jelly-roll style. Cut into strips ¼-inch wide. Uncoil. Dry on paper toweling for 10 minutes. Can be made ahead and stored in an airtight container.

To Cook

- 5 quarts water
- 3 tablespoons salt
- 3 tablespoons vegetable oil

Bring water to a boil in a large stockpot. Add salt and vegetable oil. Add noodles. Cook until just tender, 2 to 3 minutes. Drain noodles. Transfer to a heated serving platter.

Jams and Butters

Plum Jam

Makes 2 pints.

2½ pounds plums, pitted and quartered
(Leave skins on for a deep red color)
1 small seedless orange, cut in half, ends removed
½ cup water
3½ to 4½ cups granulated sugar

Insert Steel Blade

Place 2 cups of the plums in the Work Bowl; process nonstop until puréed, about 10 seconds. Place purée in a 4-quart saucepan. Process remaining plums.

Insert Slicing Disc

Fit orange halves into the bottom of the Feed Tube. Place Cover on Work Bowl. Slice with medium pressure. Add orange slices to plums.

Add water to plum mixture. Bring to a boil. Boil 10 minutes, stirring occasionally. Place thermometer in pan. Add sugar. Reduce heat to medium. Cook for 15 to 20 minutes, stirring occasionally until thermometer reaches 220°.

Pour mixture into prepared jars and seal. If using paraffin, use according to package directions. Store in refrigerator.

Blueberry-Apple Preserves

Makes 1½ pints.

2 Granny Smith apples, peeled, cored, and quartered
1 quart blueberries
1 small lemon, ends removed
¼ cup water
4 cups granulated sugar

Insert Grating Disc

Arrange apples in the Feed Tube; grate. Place apples in a 4-quart saucepan. Add blueberries.

Insert Slicing Disc

Fit lemon into the bottom of the Feed Tube. Place Cover on Work Bowl. Slice with medium pressure. Add to apples and blueberries.

Add water. Bring mixture to a boil. Reduce heat to a simmer; simmer for 10 minutes. Stir in sugar. Cook over medium heat 15 to 20 minutes or until thermometer registers 220°. (If not using thermometer, drop ½ teaspoon preserves onto a cold plate. If mixture gels, remove from heat.) Pour preserves into prepared jars. Seal according to directions. If using paraffin, use according to package directions.

English Orange Marmalade

Makes 1½ pints.

6 medium seedless oranges, halved, ends removed
1 medium lemon, ends removed
½ cup candied cherries, optional
Water
Granulated sugar

Insert Slicing Disc

Fit orange halves into the bottom of the Feed Tube. Place Cover on Work Bowl. Slice with firm pressure. Place orange slices in a large bowl. Fit lemon into the bottom of the Feed Tube; return to processor; slice with firm pressure. Remove any seeds. Add to oranges. Mix in cherries.

Measure fruit. Add 1½ cups water for each cup of fruit. Cover with plastic wrap. Refrigerate overnight.

Place fruit in a 4-quart saucepan. Simmer for 1½ hours or until the fruit is tender. If mixture is dry, add water, 2 tablespoons at a time. Cool to room temperature. Refrigerate overnight.

Measure fruit. Add 1 cup sugar for each cup of fruit. Cook over medium heat for 30 minutes or until fruit begins to gel. Pour into sterilized jars and seal. If using paraffin, use it according to package directions.

Herb Butter

Makes ¼ to ½ cup.

2 sprigs fresh parsley
3 basil leaves
1 teaspoon chives, cut into ½-inch pieces
¼ pound butter, chilled, cut into ½-inch pieces

Insert Steel Blade

Wash herbs and dry with paper toweling. Place parsley, basil, and chives in the Work Bowl; process until minced, 10 seconds. Add butter; process nonstop until thoroughly blended. Store in a covered container in the refrigerator.

Peanut or Cashew Butter

Makes 2 cups.

- 2 cups shelled and peeled, unsalted peanuts or cashews
- 2 teaspoons butter or honey

Insert Steel Blade

Place nuts and butter in the Work Bowl; pulse 5 times. Stop occasionally to scrape sides of Work Bowl. Run processor nonstop until the desired consistency.

For chunky peanut butter, set aside ½ cup of the chopped nuts. Process remaining peanuts until desired consistency. Add reserved nuts; process 2 seconds, just to combine. Store in a covered container in the refrigerator.

New England-Style Apple Butter

Makes approximately 3 pints.

- 5 pounds cooking apples, peeled, cored, and quartered
- 1½ cups cider or apple juice
- 2½ cups granulated sugar
- 3 tablespoons ground cinnamon
- 1 teaspoon ground nutmeg
- ½ teaspoon ground cloves

Insert Slicing Disc

Fit apples randomly into the Feed Tube; slice with light pressure. Remove to a 4- to 6-quart saucepan. Continue until all apples are sliced.

Add remaining ingredients to saucepan. Simmer, uncovered, for 45 minutes, stirring occasionally. Remove to a large bowl; cool.

Insert Steel Blade

Ladle 2 cups of the apples into the Work Bowl; purée. Pour into a 3-quart saucepan. Continue until apples are puréed.

Simmer for 30 minutes, stirring occasionally. Pour into sterilized jars and seal.

Garlic Butter

Makes ½ cup.

- 4 cloves garlic
- ¼ pound butter, cut into ½-inch pieces and brought to room temperature

Insert Steel Blade

With the processor running, drop garlic through the Feed Tube; process 5 seconds, until minced. Add butter to the Work Bowl; cream. Stop occasionally to scrape sides of Work Bowl. Store in a covered container in the refrigerator.

Parsley Butter

Makes ½ cup.

- 2 cloves garlic
- 4 sprigs parsley, rinsed and patted dry
- ¼ teaspoon salt
- ⅛ teaspoon white pepper
- ¼ pound butter, chilled, cut into ½-inch pieces

Insert Steel Blade

With the processor running, drop the garlic through the Feed Tube; process until the garlic is minced, about 5 seconds. Add parsley; process until minced, about 10 seconds. Scrape the sides of the Work Bowl with a rubber spatula as necessary. Add salt, pepper, and butter; process until combined. Store in a covered container in the refrigerator.

Almond Butter

Makes ½ cup.

- ⅓ cup whole almonds
- ¼ pound butter, chilled, cut into ½-inch pieces

Insert Steel Blade

Place almonds in the Work Bowl; process 10 seconds. Leave almonds in the Bowl. Add butter pieces; process until combined. Remove with rubber spatula. Store in a covered container in the refrigerator.

Lemon Butter

Makes ½ cup.

- 1 1-inch piece lemon rind
- ¼ pound butter, chilled, cut into ½-inch pieces
- 1 tablespoon lemon juice

Insert Steel Blade

Place rind in Work Bowl; process until fine. Add butter and juice; process for 6 seconds. Stop occasionally to scrape sides of Work Bowl.

Use on fish, baked potatoes, and vegetables.

Babas au Rhum

Makes 8 babas.

- ¼ cup warm water (105 to 115° F.)
- 1 package active dry yeast
- 1 teaspoon sugar
- ¼ cup milk, scalded, cooled to room temperature
- 6 tablespoons butter, cut into ½-inch pieces and brought to room temperature
- ¼ teaspoon salt
- ¼ cup sugar
- 3 eggs
- 2 cups unbleached all-purpose flour
- ½ cup cake flour

Pour water into a measuring cup. Sprinkle yeast and the 1 teaspoon sugar over water; stir to dissolve yeast. Place in a draft-free place for about 5 minutes. Combine milk, butter, and salt in a small saucepan. Heat until butter melts. Cool to room temperature.

Insert Steel Blade

Place remaining sugar and eggs in Work Bowl; process 5 seconds. Add milk and yeast mixtures; process 5 seconds. Remove cover. Add flours; process 3 seconds, just to blend.

Butter 8 baba molds (available at gourmet stores) or custard cups. Fill mold half full with batter. Cover molds with buttered aluminum foil or a damp cloth. Place dough in a warm draft-free place until it has risen to the tops of the molds, about 20 to 25 minutes. Place molds on a baking sheet. Bake for 15 minutes or until babas test done. Remove from molds and cool on a wire rack.

Syrup

- 3 cups water
- 1½ cups sugar
- ⅓ cup dark rum

Heat water and sugar in a 1½-quart saucepan until the syrup is clear, about 5 minutes. Remove from heat. Stir in the rum. Place babas on a rack over a baking sheet. Slowly drizzle syrup over babas until all syrup is absorbed.

Glaze

- 1 cup apricot jam
- 2 tablespoons sugar
- 3 tablespoons dark rum
- 8 candied cherries

Combine jam and sugar in a small saucepan.

Cook over medium heat until mixture reaches 228° F. on a candy thermometer. Stir in rum. Glaze babas with warm apricot glaze. Garnish each with a candied cherry. Refrigerate until ready to serve.

No-Bake Chocolate Mousse Cake

Makes 10 to 12 servings.

- 1 14-ounce package chocolate chip cookies
- 6 tablespoons butter, melted
- 1 12-ounce package semisweet chocolate pieces
- ½ cup strong coffee
- 2 tablespoons dark rum
- 3 jumbo egg whites, room temperature
- ¾ cup sugar
- 3 jumbo egg yolks, room temperature
- 3 cups heavy cream, chilled and whipped

Preheat oven to 350°.

Insert Steel Blade

Place half of the cookies in the Work Bowl; process until ground. Set aside. Process remaining cookies. Return all crumbs to the Work Bowl. With the machine running, pour butter through the Feed Tube. Process for 5 seconds. Remove Cover and scrape the sides of the Work Bowl with a rubber spatula. Replace Cover; process 2 seconds. Remove crumbs; do not clean Work Bowl. Press crumbs into a buttered, 9-inch springform. Bake for 5 minutes. Remove from oven and set aside to cool.

With Steel Blade in place, place chocolate in Work Bowl; chop. Pour coffee and rum into a small saucepan; bring to a boil. With the machine running, pour the hot coffee mixture through the Feed Tube. Process until the chocolate is melted. Cool in Work Bowl.

Beat egg whites with an electric mixer until soft peaks form. Sprinkle sugar, ¼ cup at a time, over egg whites, beating until stiff peaks form. Set aside. Add egg yolks to cooled chocolate mixture in Work Bowl; process about 10 seconds.

Gently fold chocolate mixture into egg whites; then fold mixture into whipped cream. Pour into prepared crust. Cover with plastic wrap. Freeze for 8 hours or overnight. Place in refrigerator 4 hours before serving. Decorate with chocolate curls, if desired.

Old-Fashioned Strawberry Cream Puffs

Makes 12 large puffs.

- 1 cup water
- ¼ teaspoon salt
- ¼ pound butter, cut into ½-inch pieces and brought to room temperature
- 1 cup all-purpose unbleached flour
- 2 tablespoons granulated sugar
- 4 eggs

Combine water, salt, and butter in a medium saucepan. Bring mixture to a boil, stirring until the butter melts. Remove saucepan from heat. Add flour and sugar; beat with a wooden spoon until the mixture pulls away from the sides of the saucepan and forms a ball.

Insert Steel Blade

Add flour mixture and 1 egg to Work Bowl; combine 3 seconds. With the processor running, drop the remaining eggs, 1 egg at a time, through the Feed Tube; process until batter is shiny and smooth.

Preheat oven to 425°. Lightly grease a large baking sheet. Drop batter by tablespoonfuls 2 inches apart onto the baking sheet. Bake for 20 minutes. Reduce heat to 350°. Bake 14 minutes or until puffs are golden brown. Remove puffs from oven. Slit the top of each puff with a knife. Turn oven off and return puffs to oven to dry. Slice off tops of puffs. Remove any uncooked dough.

While puffs are cooling, prepare Strawberry Cream Filling. Fill one hour before serving. Can also be filled and frozen.

Strawberry Cream Filling

- ½ cup confectioners' sugar
- 1 pint strawberries, hulled
- ½ pint heavy cream, whipped

Insert Steel Blade

Place sugar in Work Bowl. Pulse 4 times. Remove and set aside.

Insert Slicing Disc

Place berries alternately in Feed Tube. Slice with firm pressure. Set strawberries aside.

Fold half of the sugar into the whipped cream. Repeat with remaining sugar. Fold berries into whipped cream.

Walnut Torte

Makes 8 servings.

- 2 cups walnuts
- ¼ cup unbleached all-purpose flour
- 1 teaspoon baking powder
- ¼ teaspoon salt
- 6 extra large egg yolks, room temperature
- 1¼ cups sugar
- 6 extra large egg whites, room temperature

Lightly butter two 8-inch layer pans. Line the pans with waxed paper. Butter waxed paper. Set aside. Preheat oven to 350°.

Steel Blade

Place walnuts in Work Bowl. Grind for 10 to 15 seconds. (Processor will be noisy.) Add flour, baking powder, and salt to the nuts in the Work Bowl. Process 4 seconds. Place mixture in a large mixing bowl; set aside. Add egg yolks and sugar to the Work Bowl; process for 30 seconds. Fold egg yolk mixture into the nut mixture. Beat egg whites in a large mixing bowl until stiff peaks form. Fold egg whites into the walnut mixture. Pour batter into the prepared cake pans. Bake 25 minutes or until the cakes test done. Invert cakes on a wire rack to cool. Remove waxed paper.

To Assemble

- 1 cup heavy cream, chilled
- 5 tablespoons sugar
- 1 teaspoon vanilla

Whip cream in a large mixing bowl until soft peaks form, beating in 1 tablespoon sugar at a time. Fold in vanilla. Place one of the layers top-side up on a serving plate. Spread whipped cream over top and sides. Place the second layer, top-side down, over the bottom layer. Frost with remaining whipped cream. Chill until ready to serve.

Apricot Soufflé

Makes 8 servings.

- 1¼ cups dried apricots
- ½ cup granulated sugar
- 3 tablespoons butter
- ¼ cup unbleached all-purpose flour
- 1 cup milk
- 5 egg yolks
- 1 tablespoon orange juice
- 6 egg whites

Place apricots in a small saucepan. Cover with

water. Bring to a boil; reduce heat and simmer for 20 minutes or until tender. Drain.

Insert Steel Blade

Place the apricots in the Work Bowl. Process until puréed. Add sugar; process 5 seconds. Set aside.

Cut a collar of waxed paper or aluminum foil 2 to 3 inches higher than a 1½-quart soufflé dish. Butter one side of the waxed paper. Secure waxed paper, buttered-side in, to the soufflé dish with wooden picks. Preheat oven to 350°.

Melt the 3 tablespoons butter in a 2-quart saucepan. Whisk in flour; beat until flour is absorbed. Slowly beat in milk. Simmer and stir until mixture thickens. Remove from heat. Whisk in egg yolks, 1 at a time. Whisk in the apricot purée and orange juice. Beat egg whites with an electric mixer until stiff peaks form. Gently fold apricot mixture into the egg whites.

Pour mixture into the prepared soufflé dish. Bake for 45 minutes or until firm. Carefully remove collar. Serve immediately.

Fruit Salad Upside-Down Cake

Makes 8 servings.

- ½ cup butter
- 1¼ cups packed brown sugar
- 1 30-ounce can fruit salad, drained on paper toweling; reserve ½ cup of the juice
- 3 eggs
- 1 cup sugar
- 1 teaspoon vanilla
- 1½ cups cake flour
- ½ teaspoon salt
- 1½ teaspoons baking powder

Carefully melt butter and brown sugar in a 9-inch layer pan, stirring occasionally. Remove pan from heat when sugar begins to bubble. Spread the drained fruit over the sugar. Preheat oven to 350°.

Insert Steel Blade

Add eggs and sugar to Work Bowl; process for 6 seconds. Add reserved juice and vanilla; pulse 4 times. Add cake flour, salt, and baking powder; pulse 4 times. Pour batter over fruit. Bake for 45 minutes or until cake tests done. Cool cake in pan. Invert onto a serving platter. Serve with sweetened whipped cream.

Rum Balls

Makes 5 dozen.

- 12 ounces vanilla wafers
- 2 cups pecans
- 2 cups raisins
- 1 cup confectioners' sugar
- 2 tablespoons light corn syrup
- ¼ cup dark rum
- 1 cup granulated sugar
- 3 tablespoons cocoa

Insert Steel Blade

Lightly crumble wafers. Add about 2 cups crumbled wafers at a time to the Work Bowl; grind into crumbs, about 10 to 15 seconds. Remove to a large mixing bowl. Repeat until all wafers are processed. Set aside. Add pecans to Work Bowl; grind about 10 seconds. Add pecans to wafers.

Add raisins and confectioners' sugar to Work Bowl; process 5 seconds. Add to wafers.

Add corn syrup and rum to the wafers; mix well. Return half of the batter to Work Bowl. Process for 8 seconds; remove from Work Bowl and set aside. Repeat procedure; return all to mixing bowl. Shape into ¾-inch balls.

Combine granulated sugar and cocoa; mix lightly. Roll balls in the sugar-cocoa mixture. Store in an airtight container. Flavor improves with age.

All-Purpose Piecrust

Makes one 9- or 10-inch piecrust.

- 1½ to 1¾ cups unbleached all-purpose flour
- ⅛ teaspoon salt
- 6 tablespoons chilled butter, cut into ½-inch pieces
- 2 tablespoons vegetable shortening
- 5 to 7 tablespoons cold water

Insert Steel Blade

Place flour, salt, butter, and vegetable shortening in Work Bowl. Process until the mixture resembles coarse crumbs. With the processor running, pour the cold water through the Feed Tube. A dough ball will form.

Remove the dough ball from the processor. Wrap in waxed paper or plastic wrap. Refrigerate for 30 minutes to 1 hour before rolling out.

Pear Nut Cake

Makes 8 servings.

- ¾ cup shelled hazelnuts or walnuts
- 2 large pears, peeled, cored, and cut into 1-inch pieces
- 1 tablespoon lemon juice
- 2 teaspoons ground cinnamon
- ½ cup butter, room temperature
- 1 cup granulated sugar
- 2 eggs
- 1 cup sour cream
- 1 teaspoon vanilla
- ¼ teaspoon salt
- 1 teaspoon baking powder
- 1 teaspoon baking soda
- 2 cups unbleached all-purpose flour

Insert Steel Blade

Place nuts in Work Bowl; chop. Place nuts in a mixing bowl. Add pears to the Work Bowl; chop roughly. Add pears, lemon juice, and cinnamon to nuts; toss lightly; set aside. Add butter and sugar to the Work Bowl; process for 10 to 15 seconds. Add eggs, sour cream, and vanilla; process 10 seconds. Add salt, baking powder, baking soda, and flour; process until thoroughly blended. Butter a 9-inch square baking pan. Preheat oven to 350°. Pour batter into pan. Drop pear-nut mixture by spoonfuls over batter. Cut mixture into the batter with a knife. Bake for 45 minutes. Cool before cutting into 3-inch squares. Serve with sweetened whipped cream.

Pear Sherbet

Makes 6 servings.

- ½ cup granulated sugar
- ½ cup water
- 1 29-ounce can pears, drained, cut into ¾-inch pieces
- 4 tablespoons pear liqueur, optional
- 1 teaspoon lemon juice
- 1 cup milk

Combine sugar and water in a small saucepan. Bring mixture to a boil; boil for 3 to 4 minutes, stirring occasionally. Remove from heat. Set aside to cool.

Insert Slicing Disc

Place pears in Work Bowl; process until puréed, about 30 seconds. Add liqueur, lemon juice, and milk. Process just to combine. With machine running, pour cooled syrup through Feed Tube; process 8 seconds. Pour mixture into a baking dish. Place in the freezer until the mixture is firm.

Insert Steel Blade

Spoon mixture into the Work Bowl. Process until soft, 8 seconds. Pour into 6 individual glasses. Return to freezer. Remove from freezer 15 minutes before serving.

Perfect Cheesecake with Blueberry Topping

Makes 12 servings.

- 2 8-ounce packages cream cheese, cut into thirds and brought to room temperature
- 16 ounces cream-style cottage cheese
- 1½ cups granulated sugar
- 4 extra large eggs
- 3 tablespoons cornstarch
- 1½ tablespoons lemon juice
- 1 tablespoon vanilla
- ¼ pound butter, melted, and cooled
- 1 pint sour cream
- 1 21-ounce can blueberry pie filling

Preheat oven to 325°. Lightly butter a 9-inch springform.

Note: Process recipe in two batches and then combine.

Insert Steel Blade

Place 1 package of the cream cheese and half of the cottage cheese in the Work Bowl. Process with On-Off control or pulse technique until cheeses are combined. Add ¾ cup of the sugar, 2 of the eggs, 1½ tablespoons of the cornstarch, ¾ teaspoon of the lemon juice, ½ tablespoon of the vanilla, 4 tablespoons of the butter and 1 cup of the sour cream; process until thoroughly blended. Remove to a large mixing bowl. Repeat procedure with the remaining ingredients.

Combine the two batches of filling; pour into the prepared pan. Bake for 1 hour and 10 minutes, or until cake is firm. Turn off oven. Leave the cake in the oven for 2 hours with the oven door closed. Remove the cake from the oven. Cool completely. Refrigerate at least 6 hours before serving.

When ready to serve, run a spatula around the sides of the pan to loosen cake from pan. Remove sides of springform. Spoon blueberry pie filling over top of cake.

Perfect Cheesecake with Blueberry Topping

Index

A
B
C
D
E
F
G
H
I
K
L
M